Jennie M. Mosher

Story of the Bible in Rhyme

Jennie M. Mosher

Story of the Bible in Rhyme

ISBN/EAN: 9783337273187

Printed in Europe, USA, Canada, Australia, Japan

Cover: Foto ©Lupo / pixelio.de

More available books at **www.hansebooks.com**

MRS. JENNIE M. MOSHER.

STORY OF THE BIBLE IN RHYME

BY

MRS. JENNIE M. MOSHER

———

INDEPENDENCE BOOK CO.,
INDEPENDENCE, IOWA.

Entered according to act of Congress in the year 1894, (eighteen hundred ninety-four,) by Mrs. Jennie M. Mosher, in the office of the Librarian of Congress at Washington.

DONOHUE & HENNEBERRY,
PRINTERS AND BINDERS,
CHICAGO.

PREFACE

TO THE STORY OF THE BIBLE IN RHYME.

That all may read these lines with care
Is my earnest wish and fervent prayer.
In writing them, my only thought,
That Jesus and his love be taught
To all the world, in words so plain
That none in ignorance need remain.
And so, in rhyme, these truths so dear,
Perhaps, to some may seem more clear.
And yet, dear readers, bear in mind,
No contradictions will you find;
They're God's own precious truths sublime,
Their meaning changed not, though in rhyme.

Mrs. Jennie M. Mosher.

CONTENTS.

	Page.
The Story of Creation...	7
First sin and punishment of Adam and Eve................	8
Birth of Cain and Abel..	9
The first murder..	9
Cain is made an outcast and founds the first city	9
The Story of the Flood....................................10–	11
The Story of Abraham.....................................11–	19
Lot moves to Sodom and is captured by four Kings........	12
Sarah being barren Abraham takes Hagar to wife...........	13
Birth of Ishmael, Hagar's son.....................................	13
Birth of Isaac and Hagar and Ishmael driven from home....	14
Destruction of Sodom and Gomorrah...........................	15
Abraham called to sacrifice Isaac................................	16
Death of Sarah..	16
The Story of Isaac and Rebekah......................17–	19
Death and burial of Abraham.....................................	19
The Story of Jacob and Esau...........................20–	21
Jacob's service for a Wife.............................22–	23
Birth of Joseph..	24
Jacob leaves Laban his father-in-law and meets Esau in the desert...24–	25
Birth of Benjamin and death of Rachel........................	26
Jacob and Esau bury their father................................	26
The Story of Joseph....................................26–	33
Joseph sold to the Egyptians and becomes an interpreter of dreams...27–	28
The famine, Joseph's brothers come to Egypt to buy corn and Joseph plans to see Benjamin...............28–	29
The brothers brought to grief, Joseph reveals himself to them and sends for his father....................30–	31
Joseph settles his kindred in Goshen...........................	31
Jacob blesses Joseph's children, then blesses his own prophesies of their future and dies................................	32
Death of Joseph..	32

CONTENTS.

	Page.
David's greatest Iniquity	93–94
Nathan condemns David	84
The death of David's son by Bathsheba	94
Bathsheba's Son Solomon	95
Amnon's passion for Tamar—he is slain by Absalom's servants	95
Absalom's rebellion	96–97
Absalom slain by Joab	97
David's lamentations—he resumes the throne	98
Amasa slain by Joab	98
Battle with the Philistine Giants	99
David punished for numbering the people	99
Adonijah's ambition to succeed David	100–102
Solomon proclaimed King	100
David's burial	101
God's gift to Solomon	101
Adonijah and Joab slain	102
Solomon's great wisdom shown	103
Building the Temple	103–105
Dedication of the Temple	104
Building of Solomon's Palace	105
The Queen of Sheba visits Solomon	105
Solomon's sin	106
Israel is divided	106
Golden Images set up by Jeroboam	108
Jadon's warning	108
The Temple spoiled because of Rehoboam's sin	110
Downfall of Jeroboam	111
Asa's good reign over Judah	112–113
Ahab's wicked reign over the other tribes	113
The prophet Elijah sent to warn him	113
Miracles performed for Elijah's sake	114
Elijah persecuted by Jezebel	116
Naboth's vineyard coveted by Ahab	117
Naboth stoned to death	117
Elijah's prophecy regarding Ahab and Jezebel	117
Jehosaphat's reign	119–121
Ahaziah's reign and death	122
Elijah translated to Heaven	124

	Page.
His mantle falls on Elisha	124
Miracles wrought by Elisha	124-129
Miraculous termination of a famine	131
Prophecies of Elisha	132
The two Kingdoms contemporaneously led by Kings named Jehoram	133
Jehu anointed King	134
Terrible death of Jezebel	134
Destruction of the Worshipers of Baal	135
Two kings named Joash	136
Death of Elisha	137
Joash, king of Judah, slain by his servants	138
Azariah profanes the House of the Lord and is smitten as a Leper	139
Israel's kingdom brought to an end	141
Hezekiah's reign over Judah	141
Treachery of the Assyrian King	142
Hezekiah sends to the prophet Isaiah for counsel	143
Hezekiah's life spared fifteen years	143
Josiah's good reign	144-145
Jerusalem destroyed	146
Captivity of Judah	146
The proclamation of Cyrus for the rebuilding of the temple	147
Ezra goes to Jerusalem as a reformer	149
Nehemiah goes to Jerusalem to assist in the work of rebuilding, and while there does the work of a pious reformer	150
The Story of Esther	152-155
The Story of Job's faith	156-158
The Story of Daniel	159-166
The Fiery Furnace	161
Nebuchadnezzar an exile seven years	163
Belshazzar's feast	163
Daniel cast into a den of Lions	165
Daniel's vision	166
The Story of Jonah	166-168
Books of prophecy	168-170
The mission of John the Baptist	170
Marriage of Joseph and Mary	171

CONTENTS.

	Page
Birth of Jesus	171
An angel announces the glad tidings	172
Wise men guided by a star	173
Joseph's flight into Egypt	173
Herod murders the children of Bethlehem	174
Jesus expounding the Scriptures with the Doctors	174
Baptism of Jesus by John	175
The forty days fast and temptation	176
Preaching of John	176–177
The first miracle	177
Money changers driven from the temple	177–178
Conversion of Nicodemus	178–179
John is beheaded	180
Jesus meets the Samaritan woman at Jacob's well	181
He declares himself to be the Messiah	182
Healing of the nobleman's son	182–183
Jesus visits Nazareth	183
Miraculous draught of fishes	184
Healing a paralytic	185
The Pharisees accuse Jesus of wrong doing	186
Christ heals the cripple	187
Twelve Apostles chosen	187
The Centurion's faith rewarded	188
Jesus anointed by a penitent woman	188–189
Jesus calms the tempest	189
Devils cast out of a demoniac	190
The raising of Jairus' daughter	191
Jesus feeds the multitude	192
Jesus walks on the sea	192
Jesus the bread of life	193
Jesus foresees his betrayal and destruction	194–195
Simon Peter's confession	195
Jesus predicts his death and resurrection	195
Christ's transfiguration	195
The lunatic healed	196
Jesus questioned by his disciples	196
Healing the ten lepers	197–198
Parable of the good Samaritan	199
The woman taken in sin	200

CONTENTS.

	Page.
Blind Bartimeus healed	200
Parable of the good Shepherd	201
Raising of Lazarus	202–203
Parable of the great supper	204
Parable of the prodigal son	204–205
Parable of the rich man and Lazarus	205–206
The rich young man	206
Parable of the laborers	206–207
Zaccheus acknowledges Christ	207–208
The triumphant entry into Jerusalem	208
Parable of the Vineyard	209
The poor widow's mite	210
Parable of the ten Virgins	211
Parable of the talents	211–212
Description of the last judgment	212
Designs against the Lord's life	212
The Last Supper	213
Jesus comforting his disciples	214
Christ prayeth to his Father	215
Judas betrayeth Jesus	215
Peter's denial	216
The trial of Jesus	216–217
Remorse and suicide of Judas	218
The Crucifixion	219–220
The burial of Jesus	220
The resurrection of Christ	221
Jesus appears to Mary Magdalene	221
Mary his mother cometh to the Sepulcher	222
Jesus meets with his disciples	223
The doubts of Thomas	223
Jesus' last meeting with his Disciples	224–225
The Ascension	225
The day of Pentecost	226
First miracle of John and Peter	227
Arrest and trial of the Apostles	228
Punishment of Ananias and Sapphira	229
Seven Deacons Chosen	230
Stephen is stoned to death	230–231
Conversion of the Eunuch	232

	Page.
Conversion of Paul	233
Dorcas raised from the Dead	234
Conversion of Cornelius	234
An Angel delivered Peter from prison	235
Barnabas and Paul as Evangelists	236
Paul and Barnabas separate	238
Conversion of Lydia	239
Paul and Silas cast into Prison	239
They are released and continue to preach	240
Paul's discourse in the midst of Mars' Hill	241
Paul at Ephesus	242
Paul's trials in Jerusalem	244-245
Paul before Felix	246
Paul before Agrippa	246
Shipwreck of Paul	247
He cometh safely to land	247
Paul preaches in Rome	248
Visions of St. John on the Island of Patmos	249

STORY OF THE BIBLE IN RHYME

GENESIS.

God made this beautiful world of ours,
The sun, the moon, the grass and flowers;
He made the fishes in the sea,
The beasts and birds created he;
'Tis good, and yet again He spake—
In Our own image, let Us make
A being, unto whom shall be
All things subservient made by me.

And now the seventh day had come,
And God his labors rested from;
This day, he sanctified and blessed,
Proclaimed it as a day of rest.
Our loving Father next did give—
The man He'd formed, a place to live:
A garden beautiful and bright,
A perfect Paradise of light.

With food and water well supplied,
One thing alone, to him denied.
A certain tree of knowledge there:
God said to Adam, do not dare
The fruit to eat, for if you do
The penalty is death to you.

But that alone thou shalt not be,
A helpmeet I will give to thee.
The Lord His promise then to keep,

Caused Adam deeply sound to sleep,
And from his side a rib did take,
A woman, out of which to make.

This woman, Eve, was Adam's wife,
And changed the plan of his whole life,
For she, the serpent listened to—
Charmed with the picture that he drew;
How knowing gods, they'd surely be,
By eating fruit from off that tree,
Of which the Lord had said untruly:
To eat of it, you'll die most surely.

She ate, and to her husband gave
The fruit which did them both enslave.
No longer free from sorrow they,
For this, the Lord did to them say:
The serpent, in the dust shall crawl,
A cursed thing, despised by all.
Great pain and sorrow Eve shall heir,
The ground, shall thorns and thistles bear.

A life of toil was Adam given,
While out of Eden, both were driven,
The tree of life, that grew therein,
With flaming sword and Cherubim
Was guarded well on every side.
For having now, God's law defied,
The forfeit pay they surely must,
And die at last, return to dust.

Their work of labor well begun,
God gives them Cain, their first born son.
A tiller of the land was he,
And proved a wicked man to be.
His brother Abel tended sheep,
God's love and law he sought to keep.
They each brought offerings to the Lord,
And each received his own reward.

Cain's wicked and rebellious heart
In Abel's blessing had no part.
And so his hate and anger grew—
Until at length his brother slew.
One sinful deed leads to another:
When asked by God, Where is thy brother?
He thought his wicked deed to hide,
And thus again his Lord denied.
But God, omniscient, just and true,
Gave unto Cain his rightful due.
A vagabond he now became,
With branded brow and tarnished name.
A wanderer away from God,
He settled in the land of Nod.

And there did God prolong his life,
Permitted him to take a wife,
To build a city, children raise.
God's loving kindness all should praise.
In Enos days we read that man,
To call upon the Lord began.
This man, grandson to Adam was,
His father Seth, by nature's laws.

Enoch, a godly man, indeed,
Translated was, for so we read,
And that Methuselah, his son,
The oldest man of every one,
Was unto Noah very near,
Grandfather, so it doth appear.
But now God's heart is filled with grief,
To see man's sin and unbelief.
To destroy the world, begin anew,
Is what he plans, and has in view.
The man God chooses from the rest,
Is Noah, who of all seems best.
An ark he tells him how to build,
With living creatures to be filled.

This privilege unto Noah gave,
His wife and children he might save.
When Noah reached six hundred years,
Within the ark, so it appears,
Were all God wished on earth to stay,
The rest, the flood had washed away.
For forty days and nights it rained,
And then, by God, it was restrained.

In one hundred and fifty days 'tis stated
The waters had somewhat abated;
On Mount Ararat, the highest land,
The seventh month, the ark did stand.
A dove sent out three times before,
It returned to Noah again no more.
And now the ark is opened wide,
That every living thing inside;

Beasts, Birds, and every creeping thing,
Their work on earth again begin.

With love for God was Noah filled,
Which caused him to an altar build,
And consecrate it to his Lord,
This covenant, was his reward:
All flesh from fear of floods I'll free,
This world, no more, shall deluged be.
And lest my promise I forget,
My bow within the clouds I'll set.

In time the earth seemed filled again,
With beasts, and birds; also with men,
Whose language now was all the same,
But soon, how different it became.
For they with evil hearts began
A tower, which equal to their plan,
The top would unto heaven reach;
And so did God confound their speech.

Also, He scattered them abroad,
But unto Abram, man of God,
The land of Canaan, now gave he.
Likewise, he said, I'll make of thee—
A nation great, and thee I'll bless;
Great wealth, did Abram soon possess.

A famine came, and then he thought,
To take his wife, his nephew Lot—
With him in Egypt, there to dwell;
His wife so fair: the King pleased well.

To Pharaoh's house was Sarai brought,
She's Abram's sister, so he thought,
For Abram, fearing for his life
Had so requested of his wife.

A brother, I will seem to thee;
But God deceived, can never be.
He sent great plagues to Pharaoh—
Which forced him to let Sarai go.
Again in Canaan, settled they,
While Lot, to Jordan, went his way.
They both were very rich indeed;
But unto Abram, and his seed,
God said, as far as you can see,
The land I give it unto thee.

Once more did Abram move his tent;
This time, to Mamres plains he went:
He built an altar there straightway.
His God did reverence, day by day.
Lot's tent in Sodom, now is found;
Which did in wicked men abound;
Four wicked kings to Sodom came,
And Lot was captured by the same.

But Abram, hearing of the news,
With servants armed he them pursues,
And faithful being in their duty,
The robbers soon gave up their booty.
The king of Sodom wished to pay
Them for their service, in some way:
But Abram, kindly him refused,
Knowing 'twas God who had them used.

His maker then himself revealed—
And said, fear not, for I'm thy shield.
Encouraged, Abram then and there—
Told God how much he wished an heir:
Who answering said, of stars you see
Great numbers, so your seed shall be.

Again the Lord to him appears,
And said: thy seed four hundred years
In a strange land, shall toil and drudge,
Their persecutors, then, I'll surely judge.
But thy people free, I will elevate;
Endow them with possessions great.
To thee a good old age I'll give,
Thou shalt in peace and comfort live.

Sarai, being childless, was distressed:
A handmaid, Hagar, she possessed;
Urged by her fruitless, lonely life,
Her handmaid gave, as Abram's wife,
Who bore a son, Ishmael by name.
Sarai and Hagar now became
Estranged; and Hagar also felt
Herself by Sarai hardly dealt.

God ever loving, good and kind:
For Sarai's comfort and peace of mind,
Did unto her this fact make known,
A son I'll give thee, of thine own.
To Abram thus, he also spake:
Father of nations, thee I'll make,
Now Abraham shall be thy name,
Sarai to Sarah: changed the same.

Ishmael by Abraham was brought
Before the Lord, his blessing sought;
God kindly granted this request,
And promised Ishmael should be blest;
But Sarah's son, I'll Isaac call;
On him, shall greater blessings fall.

Isaac with love filled Sarah's heart;
Ishmael, in it, received no part;
And so to Abraham, she spake:
Let Hagar, and her son now take
Another home, away from me—
Her son, no heir with mine shall be.

Abraham, with sadness, heard her through;
His Lord then told him what to do.
Sarah's request unto take heed,
For in Isaac shall be called thy seed.
Fear not for Ishmael nor his fate,
I'll make of him a nation great.

And so was Hagar kept and guarded
Herself and son, by God rewarded.

Soon after Hagar went away,
To Abraham the Lord did say:
Two cities, Sodom, being one,
So wickedly they both have done,
To destroy them now is my intention.
But Abraham to him made mention,
Of righteous men who lived therein;
To destroy them all seems like a sin.

If finding in the city ten,
Who seemeth to be righteous men,
This favor do I ask and crave,
That then this city thou wilt save.
God granted Abraham's request,
And sent two angels there to test
The city, and its righteous men;
It seems they did not find the ten.
For now we read, to Lot they went,
Saying, by God we have been sent
To destroy this sinful, wicked city.
On thee and thine will we take pity;
And lest your family be consumed
Within this city, which is doomed,
Make haste to leave, no longer stay;
Strangely, indeed, did Lot delay.

The angels, bound to save his life,
Also his daughters' and his wife,
Did force them from the city out;
No longer now their danger doubt,
For Sodom, and Gomorrah, too,
Are fire and brimstone passing through.

Lot's wife, the Lord's commands forsook,
For she did take a backward look:
Straightway she's punished for her fault,
And changed into a pillar of salt.
Lot, and his daughters, traveling fast,
The city of Zoar they reached at last;
And there they dwelt, 'tis so believed,
Until by Abraham received.

And now God calleth, Abraham,
Who, answering, said, "Lo here I am."
Then for a test the Lord did say
Go, Abraham, and right away,
Unto a mount; an altar make;
Isaac, thy son, then thou shalt take;
Sacrifice him for burnt offering.
Abraham prepared to do this thing.
Then from his girdle drew a knife,
With which to take his dear son's life;
But his faithfulness, he now had shown,
And God determined, to make known
His loving kindness, in this way:
Upon the lad thou shalt not lay
Thine hand, he said to Abraham;
Instead, was offered up a ram.
Abraham rejoicing in God's grace,
This sacred spot, named he, Lord's place.

And now was Abraham bereft—
A lonely man, his wife had left
Her earthly home for one in Heaven;
Her age, one hundred and twenty-seven.
Abraham his life had thus far spent,
By moving here and there his tent;
And so a stranger in the land,
No place of burial had he at hand.
But the people it seems sympathetic were,
And offered him every sepulcher;
Yet Abraham chose, Machpelah cave;
So free use of it the owner gave.

Abraham, though thankful, still was just;
Thus to pay for it he felt he must,
And so four hundred shekels gave;
And buried Sarah within the cave.
This place a resting place has been
For Abraham, also his kin.

His thoughts to Isaac now were turned,
In which his marriage was concerned·
For he was well advanced in life,
And wished his son to take a wife.
Yet, it was much against his will,
A Canaanite, this place to fill;
So he sent his servant to the land
Which he had left by God's command.

And so for the City of Haran then,
His servant started with camels ten.
For most of Abraham's own kin
This city were still living in.

And just outside a well of water;
'Twas customary for the daughter,
To come at eventide, to draw.
And so this servant knew and saw,
If he would settle Isaac's fate,
At evening, by this well must wait.

He came, and thus began aright,
By asking God for oversight:
And unto him made this appeal;
While quietly his camels kneel.
Let her whom Isaac's wife shall be,
When importuned this way by me,

Give unto me a drink I pray.
Oh let this maiden, then, I say—
Most graciously for me provide,
Likewise my camels, too, beside.

The daughter of Abraham's brother's son,
The first that came, she was the one:
This maiden fair and loving too,
Most willingly the water drew.
God's hand in this, the servant sees,
Which sets him very much at ease;
And from his sacks some presents drew
The damsel gave he them unto.

Then, asked her name, and if, also,
With her to lodge he might not go:
She told him of her parentage,
To lodge him, too, she did engage:
He thanked the Lord, who'd led him there
And kept him in such tender care;
With Abraham's brethren could he find
A place more pleasing to his mind.

Rebekah kindly went before,
His welcome, that she might implore;
Her brother Laban gave to him
Free entrance to their home within:
His camels cared for, and well fed,
Then before his guest a table spread;
Who said to Laban, I will not eat
Before my errand I repeat.

But first I'll tell just who I am,
The eldest servant of Abraham;

Who being rich, and very great,
This fact to you I will now state.
On Isaac will his blessing fall;
Indeed, he now has given all
His worldly goods unto this son;
He surely is the favored one.

My master sent me here to find
A wife for Isaac, to his mind.
To return with Rebekah, I now expect:
For so the Lord, did me direct.
These parents said, if God did choose
Our daughter, we shall not refuse;
And so next day they homeward started,
Rebekah quite willingly departed.

Out in the field, at eventide,
Isaac perceives them as they ride;
The servant told him what it meant,
Therefore Rebekah with him went,
And so became his loving wife,
To live with him her natural life.
And now was Abraham thus led,
Himself, another wife to wed,
Her name, Keturah, sons gave she
To Abraham, as all may see.

Abraham's age, one hundred and seventy-five—
His time to die, did now arrive:
They laid him in the cave Machpelah,
Beside his wife—departed Sarah:
Isaac and Ishmael this did do,
Which proves they both to him were true.

Twenty years was Isaac to Rebekah wed,
Twin sons now came, of which God said:
In them, two nations you'll observe;
The eldest shall the younger serve.
Esau, a hairy man, was oldest;
Jacob the younger seemed the boldest—
His brother's birth-right and his blessing,
We find, by craft, him them possessing:

His mother helped secure the latter,
She being partial in the matter;
For Jacob a favorite was with her,
But Esau, his father did prefer.
At this time Isaac much wealth possessed,
By God he had been greatly blessed.
A famine had the land passed o'er,
Still Isaac added to his store.

For God this covenant did make
With Isaac, for his father's sake:
I'll greatly multiply thy seed;
And make thee rich and great, indeed.
Then Isaac did, that which him became,
Praised God, and called upon his name.

Esau had now two living wives:
Which saddened much his parents' lives.
And yet, his father purposed not
To take his blessing—this I wot—
From him, and give unto his brother;
But Jacob, urged on by his mother,
His father, being blind, deceived.
By this was Esau greatly grieved.

And begged his father, bless him too.
What I have done, I can't undo.
But unto Esau thus he spoke:
Although, upon thy neck a yoke,
Dominion, when thou dost it take,
Thou shalt this yoke then surely break.

But Esau's heart was filled with hate,
And only did this thing await—
His father's death, and then said he
I'll make myself forever free.
By killing him, my younger brother;
This thing being told unto his mother,
Jacob she sent from home away;
With her brother Laban bade him stay.

And then to Isaac, she thus did say,
Let Jacob, now take a wife, I pray;
But surely not a Canaanite,
For this my earthly joy would blight.
Isaac quite willingly did consent,
And so to Laban Jacob went;
His father's blessing, by him taken,
Nor was he by the Lord forsaken.

But, that leaving home he might forget,
He traveled till the sun had set;
His pillow made of stones that night,
He dreamed what seemed a vision bright.
A ladder, unto Heaven ending,
God's angels on it were descending;
And He, on it, himself above,
Showed unto Jacob there his love.

As I have been to Abraham:
So unto thee; the same I am.

Jacob awoke, saying, although unknown,
The Lord has been with me I own.
The stone, on which his head had lain,
He set it up there to remain.
And also made this vow, there, then,
If I, in peace, can come again,
And return my father's house unto,
This thing I will most surely do:
The tenth of all I have I'll give,
The Lord, my God, for him I'll live.

Again his journey he pursues,
Until at length a well he views;
Some shepherds, with their sheep were there,
He asked of them to tell him where
They lived; and then again, also,
If Laban they did ever know.

They answering said, of Haran we,
And Laban there, we often see.
Behold, comes Rachael now, his daughter,
Her father's sheep with her to water;
So Jacob assisted her and stated
How very near they were related.
Rachael was beautiful and fair,
Jacob perceived it then and there.

They'd hardly reached her home, before
Her father kissed him o'er and o'er;
And so was Jacob led to find
A home, where he was treated kind.

Ere long this bargain, he thus did make,
For seven years' labor I will take
Rachael, my cousin, whom I love,
All other women, far above.

Laban consented, but we'll see
If fair with Jacob, he proved to be.
The time arrived, Jacob did wed—
Not Rachael, but Leah, instead.
This eldest daughter was not fair,
And to cover this a veil did wear.
When Jacob saw he was deceived,
For Rachael still he mourned and grieved.

Then soon after Laban to Jacob said:
Now Rachael you may surely wed;
But seven years longer with me stay—
Thus for my daughter you will pay.
To this, Jacob at once consented,
But his uncle's fraud he yet lamented;
Rachael he loved with all his heart,
How then could Leah have a part.

But God did take on her compassion,
And showed it plainly in this fashion:
While her sister childless, she had four;
So Rachel now did her fate deplore.
Polygamy, as we can plainly see,
Was practiced then quite commonly:
A maid named Bilhah, did Rachel own,
So this plan to Jacob she made known:

My maid, for a wife, I'll give to thee,
But her children all shall belong to me.

Leah then gave her maid the same,
And a family large they soon became.
But Rachael by God was ere long blessed,
For a son named Joseph, she possessed;
God gave him as her very own,
His loving kindness thus made known.

Twenty years with Laban, Jacob stayed;
The first fourteen, for Rachael paid.
And then, by both, it was agreed,
That he the flocks should tend and feed.
The spotted ones, to be taken away,
Allowed to Jacob for his pay.
This sort, increased more than the rest
And so great numbers he possessed.

Envy then filled his uncle's heart;
But God told Jacob to depart,
His kindred, and his home to see;
My promise this, I'll be with thee.
So with all he had, this place he left,
Laban accused him then of theft;
And accordingly, him did pursue,
But God, to Laban, now spake unto.

And bade him Jacob do no harm:
These words, did Laban so alarm,
That he his children blessed, at last,
Also a covenant of peace was passed
Between them, and of stones a heap,
As witness, they did make and keep.

Jacob then traveling, angels met,
Which proved that God was with him yet.

But Esau, his brother, now he fears,
Who heads an army large, he hears;
So presents his brother to conciliate,
He sends, and then results await.
To God he prays most fervently,
From Esau's hand deliver me.

Indeed, all night, he wrestled there
With God, who answered then his prayer,
For he called him Israel, and explained
That he the victory now had gained.
So he lifted up his eyes, and then,
Esau beheld, with four hundred men.
These brothers meet, they kiss and weep,
Esau to Jacob said, let's keep
Together now, but Jacob knew,
His children small, 'twould never do.

Esau, then hurried on to Seir.
Jacob, to rest his children dear,
Some little time in Succoth spent,
And then at Shalem pitched his tent.
Of trouble here he had his share,
For Dinah, the daughter Leah bare,
A prince abducted, but to wed
This maiden, he by love was led.

And here the matter would have ended,
But Jacob's sons, being much offended,
The city spoiled, the people slew.
Their father said, when this he knew,
This thing is grievous in my sight;
For well he knew it was not right.

And now God said, to Bethel flee,
An altar make there unto me.
For here it was, where on that night,
Jacob did have a vision bright.
And so again, God comes the same,
And says, let Israel be thy name.
My covenant, I here renew.
As with thy fathers, so with you.

He marked the spot, then did depart.
But soon deep sorrow filled his heart—
Rachael, his cherished, loving wife,
For Benjamin, gave up her life.
This babe to Joseph was own brother;
So both were left without a mother.
The place to Bethlehem being near,
Rachel's remains were buried here.

Jacob soon reached his native place,
And met his father, face to face;
Isaac's days on earth being now fulfilled,
By Jacob and Esau, so 'twas willed
His body should be laid away,
So this last sad tribute they did pay.
Now Jacob in Mamre settled near,
But Esau went his way to Seir.

Jacob at this time had twelve sons:
Benjamin and Joseph, favored ones.
Joseph, the elder, a precocious lad,
A coat of many colors had.
A dreamer, too, also was he,
His brothers could not bear to see

Him favored so, and thus they planned
One day, when he was close at hand,
To kill and throw him in a pit;
But Reubin did not favor it.

So cast him in did they alive,
But soon some Ishmaelites arrive;
And unto them they Joseph sell.
This story to their father tell:
We found this coat, with blood all red.
Jacob then mourned his son as dead.
The Ishmaelites did Joseph bring
And sell to an officer of the king
In Egypt, where the Lord did care
For Joseph, and him prospered there.

Now his master's wife, infatuated,
This fact to Joseph plainly stated;
But he, to her, turned a deaf ear,
And so she made it to appear
That he had wronged, and her insulted;
This accusation thus resulted:

Joseph was into prison cast;
But God was with him to the last.
Two men in prison, each do dream,
That which to them quite grievous seem;
Their dreams to Joseph being told,
He truly does to them unfold
Their meaning, and, in turn, quoth he,
Unto the king remember me.
To one he said, thou shalt go free,
The other hanged he soon would be.

The king's butler freed, was quite contented,
For Joseph's case he ne'er presented;
Until the king did dream one night—
What none could tell to him aright.

The butler then of Joseph thought,
So now to Pharaoh, he is brought,
Who unto him his dream makes known,
Its meaning this, by Joseph shown:
Seven years of plenty there shall be,
The same of famine then you'll see.
This warning heard with unbelief,
Will cause your land to come to grief.

Pharaoh, believing all Joseph said,
Placed him, next to himself, the head.
So a ruler in the land, was he,
Before whom all did bow the knee.
His wife the daughter of a priest,
Indeed from trouble he seemed released.

And now he laid by a great store
Of food, to last seven years or more.
Seven years of plenty in the earth,
And then began to come the dearth.
When known that Egypt could supply,
All countries came there, corn to buy;
The sons of Jacob now going, too,
Joseph his brothers saw and knew.

This mighty man, they little thought
Of them, the Ishmaelites had bought.
When questioned by him, thus they said,
One brother home; another dead.

So this thought within him did arise,
I'll claim to think they come as spies;
My youngest brother I, too, must see,
And so he seemed to angry be.

The corn I'll spare, but bear in mind
The brother, you have left behind,
Must hither come, and then I'll know
What you have told me must be so.
Accordingly they went their way,
But one for surety had to stay.

When they had told their father all
Which in that land, did them befall,
He first refused to them outright,
To let Benjamin go from his sight.
But when he saw, that starve they must
Except with them, his son did trust,
He gave reluctant, his consent;
And back again these brothers went.

When Joseph saw them, this said he:
I wish them all to dine with me.
These brothers then, were sore afraid,
Fearing some trouble would be made.
The servants did them kindly use;
Joseph, to carry out the ruse,
Asked them if they did well, and thrive,
Also if their father was still alive.

His feelings then were stirred so deep,
He was forced to go away to weep;
Then ordered they should drink and eat
All by themselves, for thus 'twas mete—

As 'twas considered then, an abomination,
To meet with Jews in such relation.

At early dawn they homeward start;
Joseph was playing still a part,
For he had ordered, within Benjamin's sack,
His silver cup the steward should pack.
Likewise, the money each had paid
In his own sack was to be laid.

Ere long he bids his steward go,
And tell these men, what he doth know,
That they have evil returned for good;
Who then consented, that he should
Search out, and punish, the guilty one;
And straightway then, so was it done.

In Benjamin's sack, the cup being found,
As Joseph's servant, the lad was bound.
Now the brothers, with the steward pleaded,
But their offers all were heard unheeded.
Hoping the master might relent,
These brothers back to Joseph went.
And urged him to take them all instead;
For this news would kill their father dead.

Their father's grief, they made so plain,
Joseph, no longer could refrain;
So he ordered they be left alone,
While to his brothers himself made known.
Also unto him, drew them so near,
They saw they had no cause for fear.
Then bade them here their kindred bring,
And to tell their father everything.

How he in Egypt could come and go,
And was second to none but Pharaoh,
Who to him would offer, no resistance,
But gladly render his assistance.
Then they started out, thus reassured;
As all things needed had been procured
By Joseph, who perspectively
His father's face could almost see.

And Jacob, when the truth he learned,
To meet with Joseph he so yearned,
He had no wish to wait or stay
In the land of Canaan another day.
While on his way, God's voice he hears,
Saying, in Egypt have no fears.
A nation great I'll make of thee;
Joseph, thy son, there thou shalt see.

The land of Goshen being near,
Joseph, his kindred, settled here.
The king, well pleased, bade Joseph give
A place the best, for them to live:
God them increased and multiplied,
Joseph their earthly wants supplied.
The Egyptians, too, on him depended,
Until at last this way it ended:

They'd bartered all they had for bread,
And still they said, we must be fed.
To sell themselves next time they go,
So bought he them for Pharaoh.
Their labor now the king they give,
Reserving just enough to live—

His part a fifth, and theirs the rest;
Great wealth, of course, the king possessed.

Jacob was now one hundred and forty-seven years old,
And so unto Joseph this foretold:
I feel the time is drawing nigh
When God will call and I must die;
But in Egypt bury me not, I pray,
For I would with my fathers lay.

Before he dies, was Joseph's thought,
My sons before him shall be brought;
Manasseh first, then Ephraim next,
But Jacob, Joseph quite perplexed.
For, in his blessing, he them reversed,
In making the younger one come first.
And then his own sons together did call
For his blessing, he desired to give unto them all;
Of each one's future, he now prophesied:
God's covenant for Joseph, on this, he relied.
That Shiloh should come, through Judah, he said;
How truly all know, who the Bible have read.

They each had a fortune, some ill and some good;
In the twelve tribes of Israel, each one of them stood
As a head—but we'll leave them a spell,
For the death of their father we now have to tell.
His body embalmed, and then for his grave,
They laid him away in Machpelah cave;
A procession large did follow him there—
His kindred of course, gave to him their care.

The brethren of Joseph began now to fear
Their brother no longer would be to them near;
So, for the evil they had unto him wrought,
For his love and forgiveness they earnestly sought.
He said to them, fear not, you have my good will,
I'll love and protect you, and nourish you still.
Joseph was permitted, his great grandchildren to see;
For we read, they were reared upon his own knee.
Then, dying, to the sons of Israel he said,
Some day from this land you all will be led.

His body embalmed, they laid safely away
In a coffin in Egypt that there it might stay
Until the time came, as God had decreed,
The children of Israel were to be freed;
Inherit the land, which God freely did give,
For Abraham and his seed together to live.

EXODUS.

Joseph now dead, his brothers still live
In the land which Pharaoh did unto them give.
They tended their flocks, great numbers became;
Until the Hebrew nation was mighty in name.
But now a new king in Egypt arose,
Who determined these Israelites to subdue and oppose.
But still they increased to such an extent,
To lessen their numbers in some way he meant.

And so he required of all the midwives,
When male babies came, to destroy their lives.

These women, God fearing, to do this refuse;
And so wisely manage, the king doth them excuse.
But upon his own people, then had this law passed,
Into the river alive, these boys must be cast.

A daughter of Levi, now having a son,
When three months old, caused this to be done:
An ark of bulrushes, was watertight made,
And soon after the babe within it was laid.
Some flags, by the river, luxuriantly grew,
The king's daughter bathes there, the mother well knew.

So then to this place, the ark being brought,
The princess discovered it, just as she thought.
And unto the child's sister, *this* privilege gave,
Of finding a nurse; that its life she might save.
This nurse, of course, was the child's own mother.
For how could the sister employ any other?
But the mother, in time, the child did bring
To live with the daughter of the king.

The child called Moses, when full grown,
His nationality being unto him known,
Saw an Egyptian treating a Hebrew ill,
And to avenge his people, did the Egyptian kill.
Then the king was told, and so straightway,
Declared that Moses, he now would slay.
Who, to escape this fate, unto Midian fled,
Where the daughter of a priest he very soon wed.

Now Moses, at Horeb, saw one day
A bush, which burning, yet did stay.

So he turned aside, his mind in doubt;
When God in the midst of it called out
His name. He answered promptly: here am I.
God warned him now not to draw nigh.

Take off thy shoes, his next command:
'Tis Holy ground, where thou doth stand.
As thy father's God, I can hear and see
My people in Egypt cry unto me;
And I am come to bring them where
The land doth milk and honey bear.

Now thee I'll send, with thee I'll be,
And thou shalt say, *I Am* sent me,
To the elders of Israel; say unto them, too,
The God of thy fathers is pitying you.
Then go to the king, his consent try to get
A journey to take, three days you must set.
I'm sure he won't let you, and then,
Egypt I'll smite, again and again;
After which with my help, you from them shall go,
But 'twill not be empty—this thing I well know.

How strange that Moses should hesitate,
But still he did, and further wait,
Till God great wonders let him do,
That all might know his words were true;
Also that God was to him near—
The God to Abraham so dear.

But now, said Moses, I'm slow of speech;
God answering, said, I will thee teach.
Yet Moses still urged him send another.
So Aaron went, who was his brother;

And also Moses, who was told by God,
Be sure and take with thee this rod,
That with it wonders you may do;—
His wife and sons went with him too.

To the children of Israel, first they go,
Then immediately after to king Pharaoh,
To ask of him, by God's command,
Let Israel go from out this land.
But he in anger them refused.
And the Israelites likewise abused.
Said God, by judgments now I'll bring
My people from this wicked king.

I *have* been known as God; but now
Before Jehovah they all must bow.
He said to Moses let Aaron take
This rod, which will a serpent make.
The king his wise men then did call,
And their rods became as serpents all;
But now a miracle there followed,
For they were all by Aaron's swallowed.

Soon after this, the Egyptians learned,
The waters all to blood were turned.
But Pharaoh's heart being hardened still,
God said to Moses, now my will
That Egypt shall with frogs abound,
In everything shall they be found.

Then Moses and Aaron, the king did meet;
Who begged they would the Lord entreat,
To drive the frogs from them away;
The Israelites, then go they may.

But when performed by God *his* part,
Then hard again grows Pharaoh's heart.
And now was Moses told by God,
Again let Aaron stretch forth his rod.

He did; and then within a trice,
All things were covered o'er with lice.
The magicians tried, but this time failed,
Then said, by God we are assailed.
And now again does God repeat,
Go unto Pharaoh, and entreat;
And if his heart seems hardened still,
Say unto him, God surely will
Send swarms of flies, which are immense;
But from the Israelites he'll drive them hence.

And so they come, and the king doth say,
Now deliver us, and go thy way;
But when delivered, as before,
His heart was hardened more and more.
The cattle in Egypt, next, all dead—
Not one in Goshen, for so God said.
And then a miracle was wrought,
Which boils upon the Egyptians brought.

And now to Moses God did say,
If Pharaoh yet doth answer nay,
I'll send a pestilence to kill
All those who, warned, do doubt me still.
And so the fire and hail destroyed
All who, within the fields employed,
The warning heard, and heeded not;
O, sinful man, hard is thy lot.

Then Pharaoh again seemed to relent,
And so for Moses and Aaron sent,
To entreat the Lord and then depart:
But hard as stone was yet his heart.
God said to Moses, thus I do,
To prove to Pharaoh and to you,
That I am God, none else beside—
And so the people again were tried.

This time the locusts covered the earth,
Whose ravages soon caused a dearth,
The king, alarmed, he then did make,
To Moses, another promise to break.
And now thick darkness in the land,
So dark, that none could walk or stand;
But Israel's children, all had light,
Except, as usual, in the night.

Then the king said go, but, bear in mind,
Your flocks and herds you'll leave behind.
Said Moses, nay, this will not do;
When we depart, our flocks go too.
God said, another plague I'll send,
Then Israel's bondage here will end.
All first born in the land shall die,
Even to Pharaoh, now, shall cry.

But mark with blood each Hebrew door,
That Israel I may then pass o'er.
'Twas night in Egypt; what a cry—
For one in every house did die.
The king now wished with all his heart,
For the children of Israel, at once, to start.

They went, and took all they possessed;
With gold and silver among the rest.
This last, the Egyptians to them loaned,
God meant by them it should be owned.

Four hundred and thirty years we read,
They passed in Egypt, as God decreed;
This Passover day, they commemorate
As the one when God did them liberate.
Nor did he leave them to go alone;
That he is with them, is plainly shown;
In the wilderness, as they wend their way,
A pillar of cloud they see by day;
And before them to make their pathway light,
God sends a pillar of fire by night.

But it seems the Egyptians soon repent
That the Israelites away were sent;
So, with an army large, they them pursue—
'Twas by the Red sea, they came in view.
But God told Moses just what to do,
That now this sea they might pass through.

When the Egyptians saw the waters divide,
Then boldly in they, too, did ride.
God saw the Israelites safely through,
And then the waters together he drew.
So king Pharaoh and his hosts were drowned,
Not one of their number, alive being found;
And now the Israelites sing and praise
The Lord, for his wonderful works and ways.

But when in the wilderness of Shur,
Where the waters exceedingly bitter were,

Three days for better, they searched in vain,
And then unto Moses began to complain.
So he cried to God, Him did entreat,
To make the waters of Marah sweet.
Who showed to him then a certain tree—
Cast in, and the waters sweet will be.

Twelve wells of water, and ten palm trees.
They found at Elim, and encamped by these.
After which their journey again resumed
But now their bread is all consumed.
And so in the wilderness of Sin,
To murmer at Moses they again begin.
Then God caused bread to rain from Heaven,
And quails to cover the ground at even.

This food, called manna, proved to be
Each morning, for them, a sufficiency,
Except the Sabbath, when the ground was bare,
But the day before came a double share ;
Notwithstanding this, they Moses chide,
As soon as water is again denied.
This time was Moses told by God
To go to Horeb, with his rod,
Smite there a rock, to quench your thirst,
For water freely shall from it burst.

And now with Amalek they meet,
When fight they must, or else retreat.
Moses to Joshua gave command,
While he stood up, with rod in hand,
And when his hands had heavy grown,
They sat him down upon a stone,

Aaron and Hur his hands sustained,
And thus by them was the victory gained.

Now Moses' wife and his sons also,
Lived with her father, called Jethro;
Hearing of Moses and his fame,
To the mount of God we read they came.
Jethro, a priest, was pleased to hear,
That God to Moses seemed so near:

And so with him he did advise,
Then unto God made sacrifice;
And then, by mutual consent,
Jethro again his own way went.

Three months in the wilderness passed by,
When Moses, at the foot of Mount Sinai,
This message did from God receive:
If Israel will on the Lord believe,
Above all people, they shall be
A peculiar treasure unto me.

To his people, Moses went straightway,
Who promised now the Lord to obey.
God said, three days from now I'll be
On Mount Sinai, and the people see.
And so he came, in cloud and smoke,
While unto Moses this he spoke:
Let not thy people the mount come nigh,
For if they do, they then must die.

But thou and Aaron shall come to me,
That I the law may give to thee.
There many things, God told him then,
Among the rest, the commandments ten;

Then, afterward, he goes alone,
The commandments received, on tables of stone.

The people of Moses had been content,
To stay with Aaron, when before he went;
But this last time, he goes and stays
On the mount with God for forty days.
Who said, from Israel, an offering take,
That with it a sanctuary you may make;
Also an ark, with gold o'erlay;
The work he ordered would take many a day.

Among other things that he requested,
Was that Aaron and all his sons be vested—
As priests; and with the holy oil anointed,
For now God's ministers were they appointed;
At last when their communing ends,
Moses, the mountain alone descends.

Two tables of stone this time he takes;
As a written testimony them God makes.
Also he takes a saddened heart:
For this to him doth God impart,
The Israelites, my laws have spurned;
For idolaters, they have all turned.

Now Moses for them, God importuned,
Otherwise, they would have been consumed.
But when he saw the golden calf,
And heard his people sing and laugh,
His anger then was so intense,
The tables of stone from him threw hence.

Beneath the mount, he did them break;
The golden calf, at the same time, take

And burn, while Aaron unto Moses, all in vain,
For the acts of the people sought to explain:
But within the gate, Moses stood and cried,
Come unto *me*, who's on the Lord's side?

The sons of Levi came every one;
When Moses said, let this be done,
Go out prepared to punish and slay
These men, that did not God obey.
And so that day three thousand fell,
While to the remaining ones, did Moses tell:
I'll go to the Lord, and him beseech,
Perhaps I may his mercy reach.

We know that Moses had God's grace,
For he now spake unto him, face to face:
And urged him to hasten, and soon be going,
To that land with milk and honey flowing.
He said, two tables of stone I'll make,
The same as the first, that thou didst break.
Again on the mountain, with God, he stays,
And fasts and communes for forty days.

With the tables of stone he then returns,
To teach his brethren what he there learns;
But his face did shine, and look so bright,
They turned away from him in fright.
But when he called, they ceased to fear;
Came unto him, his words to hear.
He told them many things to do,
And that if to God they would prove true,
He'd do for them the same and more
Than he had ever done before.

LEVITICUS.

The law of God's statutes, he establishes now;
And explains unto Moses, to keep them, just how.
Then bade him the children of Israel tell—
But Aaron's two sons were first to rebel.
Strange fires they offered, thus daring the Lord,
So death by fire was then their reward.

And now, after this, one of the tribe of Dan,
Blasphemed and cursed; this wicked man
Was stoned, by God's command 'twas done.
Also 'twas decreed, that now every one
Should die by stoning, just the same,
Who dared to take in vain God's name.

NUMBERS.

The Israelites in the wilderness had been two years,
When God said to Moses—so it appears—
Number the people, aged twenty and more,
But the tribe of Levi, pass them o'er.
Exempt from battle and labor, too;
This work alone the Levites shall do:

To move the Tabernacle, and for it care,
A sacred calling, for it was there
God's divine favor was made manifest;
And when a cloud on it did rest,
'Twas set up then, and all did stay
Till the cloud from o'er it passed away.

Fourteen hundred and ninety years B. C.—
We read that Bible students agree—
The number of Israelites recorded then,
Was over six hundred thousand men.

God ordered the Levites to be purified,
Strong drink was especially to them denied;
And commanded Moses, that nothing vile,
His Holy Sanctuary should defile.

But now the time is drawing nigh,
When the children of Israel leave Sinai;
To a place called Paran they all went,
The cloud showed plainly so 'twas meant.
With manna they were well supplied,
But now for meat they loudly cried.
Said Moses then, in deep despair,
How long must I this burden bear?

So God sent quails, in numbers vast:
But punished them sorely at the last,
For to eat their food they scarcely try,
Before great numbers of them die;
But soon from Paran to Kadesh they went.
And now twelve spies by God were sent,
The land of Canaan to survey;
This report made Caleb and Joshua.

The land so fruitful and so fair,
Let's haste away and settle there.
The other ten, this story told:
Great giants there did we behold.
If we were there and in their power,
These cannibals would us devour.

Moses and Aaron, with doubts, this heard,
But the Israelites believed it every word;
Caleb and Joshua, first they blamed,
Then Moses and Aaron were also named;

They threatened at last to stone these four;
Then Moses and Aaron did God implore,
His mercy, for these wicked men,
Who promised not to destroy them then.

But this, their punishment should be;
The land of Canaan, none shall see,
For in this wilderness shall die,
All those who did me sorely try;
And in this place they all must stay,
Until forty years have passed away.
For in that time by God 'twas said:
Those wicked ones should all be dead.

When the Israelites were told their sentence,
They manifested very great repentance;
But soon, their own self-will did show,
By planning now straightway to go
And take the land against God's will.
Moses, a father to them still,
Said if you go, you'll come to grief,
But they, being filled with unbelief,
This warning heeded not, but went,
And soon defeated, back were sent.

The rebellion next, by a Levite was led:
'Twas not enough that God had said,
The holy things shall be your care;
But in the priesthood they wished to share.
So a goodly number they employ,
That Aaron and Moses they might destroy,
But God by an earthquake them defeated,
Notwithstanding Moses had for them entreated.

Some killed by pestilence, and some by fire:
Were among the numbers who did conspire.
And now a miracle was wrought,
That the Israelites might all be taught—
That Aaron was by God appointed
As Holy priest to be anointed:
Twelve rods, each represent a tribe,
A name, God said, on each inscribe;
One rod shall blossom; this will be
A proof, which every one can see.

These rods, safe in the Tabernacle lay,
And examine them all the following day.
On Aaron's rod, although not a tree,
Buds, blossoms, fruit they plainly see.
Said God, in the tabernacle, lay it away,
And there as a testimony let it stay.

But now, at Kadesh, some time they'd been,
And so they went to the desert of Zin,
Where they search for water all in vain,
And so unto Aaron and Moses complain;
They both this time did God implore,
Who met them then at the tabernacle door,
And directed them, a rock to seek;
With rod in hand unto it speak.

They found the rock, but irritated,
Did contrary to what God stated.
Moses the rock struck with his rod,
The water came, but this said God:
Those under twenty, as you all well know,
To the land of Canaan will sometime go.

I designed by you, they should be led,
But this I tell you now instead.

Put Aaron's clothes upon his son,
For, as priest, Eleazer is now the one.
So Aaron then died, in the mountain Hor,
And Moses, his punishment, waited for.
But the Israelites soon leave behind,
This place, another one to find;
As wanderers, they find no peace,
Nor will their grumblings ever cease.
They cry for water, and for food,
Their manna seems not to them good.

They with God and Moses both find fault,
And in punishment for this assault,
Fiery serpents are among them sent;
Of their wickedness they now repent.
And beg of Moses to for them pray,
That God will take these serpents away.

In answer, God a remedy gave,
The people's lives whereby to save.
Telling Moses, a serpent of brass to make,
Then place it high upon a stake,
And when bitten, every person sure,
Must look at the serpent for a cure.

While traveling about, the Israelites
Came near to the lands of the Amonites,
Who refused their country, to pass through;
And so a battle, did there ensue.
But the Israelites the victory gained,
So in this land for a time remained.

And their wanderings, when they next began,
Took them to a place then called Bashan.
There the king refused them egress too,
And with an army large, did them pursue;
This king called Og, and his people all,
By the children of Israel were made to fall.

They now considerable land possessed,
Were looking forward to a day of rest;
For the forty years had near passed by,
And unto Canaan they were drawing nigh;
On Moab's plains, near Jericho,
Is the place they are destined now to go.

The Midian chiefs and the Moabites
Are much in fear of the Israelites;
Balak, who now, was the Moabite king,
Sent messengers, a prophet to bring,
As their faith in Balaam was very great,
They believed at once he'd decide their fate.

So to hire him to curse this people, they seek;
And Balaam, a Godly man, yet weak,
Instead of refusing them outright,
Asked time to think of it, over night.
God plainly told him he must not go,
For this people are blest by me, you know;
So he answered the messengers nay, but then,
Did King Balak send, still others again;
When petitioned, said God, now go you may,
But what I order, that only you'll say.

Therefore, the next morning, Balaam departed,
But had not got much more than started,

Before an angel blocked up his path,
He saw it not, but it kindled his wrath
When his beast shied out again and again;
The last time laid quite down, and then
So angry was Balaam, he beat her so—
Until God at last, himself to show,
Gave unto the beast, the power of speech.
But still the miracle failed to teach
To Balaam what by God was meant,
Till he again, the angel sent
With sword in hand, in the very same place;
Balaam then fell flat down on his face,
And begged that home he might now go,
But the angel was led to answer him no.

For God intended that Balaam now should
To the Israelite children work out some good.
Three times did Balak with Balaam plead,
But the Lord, each time, did intercede;
So the Israelites he could not curse,
But was compelled to do quite the reverse.

So Balak did then the prophet upbraid,
Who said, I have the Lord obeyed;
The words were not of my own mind,
But such as God was pleased to find;
Although baffled, Balak still was bent
On destroying the Israelites, so he sent
Idolaters and women fair;
That the Israelites they might ensnare.

To follow them, they seemed well pleased,
Till a plague great numbers of them seized;

This plague by Phineas was stayed;
Then he a priest by God was made.
Phineas to Eleazer, was his own son;
God said the priesthood through his race should run.
For he, being zealous in upbuilding God's cause,
Punished the Israelites when breaking his laws.
Twenty-four thousand Israelites the plague did take,
Before 'twas stayed for Phineas' sake.

Now God told Moses another census to take,
Of those above twenty who would warriors make.
It was found there were eight hundred and twenty more,
When the census was taken, thirty-eight years before.
Joshua, Eleazer the priest consecrated
As successor to Moses, who, as predestinated,
Would soon be called from earth away:
As all had been, save Caleb and Joshua,
Of those who had twenty years passed by,
When numbered before, at Sinai.

The Israelites, now by God directed,
An army of warriors together collected,
The Midianites thus, to meet and assault,
And punish them for their wicked fault,
When Balak, and Balaam, it doth seem,
For Israel's ruin did both plot and scheme.

This battle was long, and furious too;
But when, at last, they had fought it through,

The Israelite army, it was ascertained,
Most gloriously had the victory gained.
Five Midian kings, and the prophet Balaam too,
Were among the numbers that they slew.
Also the entire country, more or less,
East of the Jordan, they now possess.

DEUTERONOMY.

The death of Moses, being now near at hand,
God permits him to view the promised land.
But before the land he views, however,
He calls his people all together.
Recalls to mind, how oft in sin,
Long suffering God has to them been.

But while uttering much of prophecy,
He advised and warned them lovingly.
Then sang a song, under inspiration,
To learn it, was his adjuration.
Also gave them a book, in his laws abounding,
To be placed in the ark, for the Levites' expounding.
Then went from Nebo, to Pisgah's heights,
To view the inheritance of the Israelites.

When this survey was by him made,
Then the hand of death was on him laid.
He was buried by God, so it appears,
At the age of one hundred and twenty years.
His sepulcher is still unknown,
Save unto God, by him alone.

JOSHUA.

The leadership of Israel now Joshua took—
For his ancestors back, to Joseph, we'll look;

His age, at this time, was about eighty-three;
God promised his helper ever to be,
And told him, the Israelites over the Jordan to lead,
To the land he had promised to Abraham's seed.
The city of Jericho, richest and best;
The strength of its forces he decided to test.

Two spies to the city first Joshua sent,
To the house of a dissolute woman they went.
This woman, called Rahab, dare not to betray
These men to the king, or send them away.
She believed that this people by God had been led,
That they were his chosen, she had oft heard it said.
But the officers learned of their presence, and then
They ordered Rahab to deliver the men.

So the woman untruthfully these words did say,
They've been here, but now have gone on their way;
The spies until dark, she safely concealed,
And before they departed this to them revealed:
The Canaanites all do well understand,
That the Lord has given your people this land.
We've heard of the miracles, the victories won,
This land when you enter we're surely undone.

From the officers' hands I have saved you to-day,
In return, this favor I ask for my pay:
When the Israelites come to Canaan to live,
Protection unto my kindred, you'll give.
This promised, and then she lowered them down,
By a line through the window, into the town;

Which was left by agreement, for this same scarlet line,
For her future protection, was to be as a sign.

Three days in the mountains, and then they returned,
And related to Joshua all they had learned.
So to the Jordan all went the very next day,
There set up the ark, a short time to stay.
For Joshua followed not a way of his own,
But waited for God himself to make known.

Which he did, by performing a miracle there,
He ordered the priests, which did the ark bear,
To step into the Jordan, though the waters were deep,
Their feet remained dry, for they stood on a heap.
Then the Israelites all, went through on dry land,
And immediately Joshua gave this command:
One man from each tribe, a stone you must get
From the midst of the Jordan, the land is dry yet.

These twelve stones, a memorial ever shall be;
They were placed at Gilgal for their children to see.
Twelve stones were placed in the Jordan also,
Then the waters again together did flow.
That night, at Gilgal, the Israelites slept,
And then the next day the passover kept.

The city of Jericho by a wall was enclosed;
The manner of entrance an angel disclosed.
Once a day, the city you must march all around,
Six days in succession, all here must be found.

The ark always with you, great is the need,
Seven priests immediately it shall precede.
Each priest, a trumpet, in his hands shall be laid,
And out of a ram's horn they all must be made.

Then the angel to Joshua spake and did say,
Seven times all around, you must march the seventh day;
The people will shout when it comes to the last,
And the priests on the trumpet shall blow a big blast;
Then flat on the ground will come down the wall,
That the children of Israel may pass through it all.

The city is entered, and soon overthrown,
Rahab and her kindred, they save them alone;
The silver, the gold, the iron and the brass,
Into the Lord's treasury they all of it pass;
The rest of the city they destroyed by fire,
But what to do next they began to inquire;
So the country of Ai some now went to view,
Who reported the people there to be few.

No trouble was here by them apprehended,
But God, upon whom their success all depended;
For a sin at Jericho one had committed,
Ordained at Ai, they should be discomfited.
Then said unto Joshua, yourselves sanctify,
The transgressor and family must very soon die.

Although the Israelites' loss at Ai was small,
The defeat, nevertheless, did them greatly appall;
But this people, God's chosen, he intended to save,
And the victories promised he unto them gave.

At Ai, a conquest they very soon make,
The cattle and spoil of the city then take;
For so did God order, and by his desire,
The rest of the city they destroyed by fire.

Now the kings all about, realizing their fate,
Bring their forces together, and thus consolidate.
The Gibeonites entered not into the league,
But resorted to cunning, deceit and intrigue;
A few of their numbers as travelers came
To consult with God's people, they're tired and lame.

So long have they been without food or rest,
Surely, thought Joshua, they ought to be blest.
So promised to save them, without further thought,
Instead of consulting with God as he ought.
The city of Gibeon, they next plan to take,
And immediately Joshua sees his mistake.

Those travel-worn strangers in Gibeon live,
Who remind him of the protection he promised to give.
So the lives of these people, he could not then take,
But unto the Israelites he did them slaves make.
When the Amorites learn of this Gibeon affair,
To destroy them five kings with their armies prepare.

The Gibeonites then, unto the Israelites cry,
Come help us, if not, we surely must die.
God said unto Joshua go without fear,
The enemy before you shall all disappear.
His promise as ever, was strictly fulfilled,
For the Amorite army was every one killed.

Many battles were fought, and kings thirty-one,
Were conquered, before the fighting was done;
And the land, so long promised, to Israel came,
Which was promised to Abraham, also the same;
Much land to be taken still yet there remained,
Before full possession the Israelites gained.

But Joshua's work was now nearly completed,
Seven nations, west of Jordan, by him were defeated;
The Canaanites, Amorites, Hittites, Perizzites,
The Hivites, Jebusites, likewise the Girgashites.
The rest of the land, God now promised to give,
But said unto Joshua, not long shalt thou live.

To divide among Israel, all of these lands,
Is the work I now give into your hands.
Joseph's inheritance, his sons shall divide,
Ephraim and Manasseh, there's no others beside.
Two tribes and a half their portions now had,
'Twas Manasseh, and Reuben, another called Gad.
East of the Jordan, their possessions all lay,
For so ordered Moses, and him they obey.

By allotment, the division Joshua made,
But no land to the Levites was there conveyed.
God said, to the priesthood are they consecrated,
Their inheritance to Jehovah is thus purely related.
Some cities, wherein these people may live—
No other possessions to them shalt thou give.

The land about Hebron, Caleb requested;
For as a spy with Joshua he had been tested.

And not only promised this land he should see,
But his children of a portion owners should be.
Accordingly Joshua Hebron him gave;
Likewise for himself a portion did save.

And now realizing his earthly career
To a close was drawing, each day very near,
He called all the people, as Moses had done,
And adjured them to keep those laws, every one,
Which Moses had written, with God as his guide;
This God upon whom he had ever relied.

They promised obedience, unto God they would cleave,
All false gods and idols for Him would they leave.
This covenant made, that they might not forget,
Under an oak tree, a large stone was set.

Soon after Joshua died and was laid
Where the land in dividing his own had been made.
Then the high priest, Eleazer, sickened and died,
His beloved son Phineas he was buried beside.

JUDGES.

A large portion of Palestine being yet unsubdued,
The children of Israel are not through with the feud;
For the lands though divided some tribes can not own,
Until the possessors have been overthrown.
Had they served the true God, as they promised to do,
He would safely have kept them all the way through.

But when the people of Joshua's age were all dead,
Into idolatry and sin this people were led.

It seems that Joshua this trouble foresaw,
And so they were strictly forbidden by law,
With the people of Palestine, to ever affiliate;
But this injunction unheeded, did at last terminate
In driving the children of Israel away
From the God they had promised to love and obey.

This punishment, God, then upon them did bring,
They were beaten in battle by Mesopotamia's king.
Eight years as slaves, they suffer and groan,
Then learn the true God can help them alone;
For deliverance now, to him they appeal,
He sent them a leader, whose name was Othniel.

A brother to Caleb, God-fearing was he,
From the bondage of slavery, the Israelites free;
By subduing the people, who did them enslave,
Peace unto his countrymen, forty years gave;
Othniel then dying, the Israelites stray
From the God of their Fathers a very long way.
Who allowed them again to be subjugated,
And as slaves, eighteen years, for freedom they waited.

Then a Benjaminite, Ehud, being his name,
This time, a deliverer, unto them became;
The Moabite king, he by strategy killed,
Then, soon after, the rest of his mission fulfilled.
For ten thousand men in Moab were slain,
So peace for a time among them did reign.

The next fighting done, was by Shamgar alone,
And by him, the Philistines, were all overthrown
With an ox-goad, six hundred, he killed them outright,
And the entire army were then put to flight.
But now we will take a brief backward glance,
Before with our story we farther advance
The Benjaminites, as Jacob their father foretold,
In sin and bestiality had grown very bold,
Until at a period, the exact time not given,
To punish them sorely, were the Israelites driven.

In a town called Gibeah, their possessions did lie,
And a Levite in traveling, passed them close by.
They abused and insulted this man and his wife,
Outraged the poor woman, and deprived her of life.
When Israel hearing of the Levite's sad fate,
Determined the Benjaminites to utterly exterminate.

Accordingly, twenty-five thousand were slain,
And six hundred alive, are all that remain.
In less than a century, this tribe very near
As great as before, doth seem and appear;
Although severely punished, God desired them to be,
But to suppress them entirely was not his decree.

And now unto Ehud, again let us return;
The second judge of Israel, of him we learn,
That eighty years previous to his decease,
The Israelites enjoyed both liberty and peace.
But after his death, they immediately begin
To wander away into folly and sin.

And so God humbles them again in this way;
Twenty years king Jabin, as slaves, they obey.
This king's army was large; his general by name
Sisera, a wonderful man of great fame.
In addition to this, they also parade
Nine hundred chariots, of iron all made.

But all of this greatness with God to command,
Was scattered as easy as the light drifting sand.
To judge them, Deborah, the Israelites last chose,
And as deliverer now this prophetess arose,
Who, instructed by God, left no duty undone,
Until the Midianite army was slain every one.

Sisera, the great general, from the battle withdrew;
But Barak an Israelite, did him pursue
To the tent of a Kenite, he found him there dead;
With a tent pin driven all the way through his head.
And thus did Sisera depart from this life
By the efforts of Jael, the Kenite's own wife.

Then Deborah and Barak, both sing, and God praise,
For the victory gained, and his wonderful ways.
So forty years in the land doth peace again reign;
Then the Israelites turn from God in disdain.
False gods were set up, and worshipped also,
Until God his omnipotence did unto them show.

So completely their enemies hold them in sway,
To the caves, and the mountains, they flee and there stay.
Also seven years of starvation cause many to die;
And now for God's help they most earnestly cry.

Of the tribe of Manasseh was Gideon brave,
God selected him now to Israel save.

Some corn he was threshing, in secret, one day,
Lest the Midianites, seeing, would take it away.
When an angel he saw sitting under a tree,
Who saluted him thus, surely, God is with thee.
An offering before it was by Gideon brought,
'Twas devoured by fire, the meaning he thought,
God wishes my service, and so I'll inquire
Of the angel, what further the Lord doth desire.

His mission then plainly unto him was made known,
The idol of Baal must be *first* overthrown;
To deliver Israel from their enemies then
From out of three tribes call together the men.
Now the opposing army, when first Gideon saw,
Faint hearted, he almost wished to withdraw.
But before he decided his place to resign,
He called upon God to give him a sign
That he, as a leader, was now meant to be,
And so then a miracle was permitted to see.

For a fleece of wool, when there was no dew,
With water was saturated, entirely through.
Then, again, the fleece was perfectly dry,
When the dew around it all over did lie.
Then Gideon marched against this army so great,
For to conquer, he knew, would now be his fate.
But God, then desiring, his power farther to show,
Ordered the doubting ones homeward should go.
This plan revealed cowardice, unto all plain,
For only ten thousand now did remain.

But again, the army diminished must be,
For God a miracle wished them to see.
Thus, he ordered Gideon, his army to take—
Unto a certain stream, their thirst there to slake.
Where three hundred only, of those in this band,
For a drinking cup thought of using their hand.

The rest, of nothing beside, seemed to think,
Than kneeling down, that they might get a drink.
Those lapping from their hands God saw fit to choose,
And declared that the rest he would not now use.
To Gideon, three hundred, seemed a number too small,
And yet, 'twas impossible for this army to fall;
Being led by God, underneath his strong arm;
Furthermore, he had promised to Gideon no harm.

The first assault made, was arranged for the night;
Dark lanterns intended, to be all their light.
These lanterns were torches, by pitchers concealed;
The pitchers when broken, the lights were revealed.
A blast on a trumpet, and then a great shout;
All together, 'twas thought, 'twould the enemy rout.

This singular attack, as Gideon thought,
Accomplished far more than a great battle fought.
But before the enemy, were subdued, every one,
Reinforcements came, and some fighting was done.
The Israelites delivered to Gideon, bring
This offer that he shall serve them as king:
But to the law of Moses, he appeared to be true,
For he answered, Jehovah must rule over you.

But in time, notwithstanding God's miraculous aid.
We learn that Gideon away from him strayed.

As Israel's judge, we find he ruled forty years;
And no war in that time recorded appears.
But soon after his death, the Israelites spurn
The God of their fathers, and to Baalim return;
Of Abimelech his son, a king they now make;
Who wickedly the lives of his brothers all take.

His reign throughout, brought only strife and turmoil,
But his sins all at last, on his own head recoil.
His ignoble death, was lamented by none;
So in part, was he punished, for the deeds he had done.
After this, the wars for a century cease;
And the Israelites though sinful, live in comparative peace.

God, long suffering, however, determined at last,
To punish these people, for the sins of the past.
Eighteen years, by two nations, were they subjugated;
When they cried unto God, all their trials related.
But he for awhile, seemed to cast them away;
And said, to your idols for help you may pray.
Thus rebuked, their idols they break and despise;
God mercifully listened then unto their cries.

As a leader, now Jephthah, was unto them given;
For the sins of his parents, from home he'd been driven.

This wrong he resented, and was inclined to refuse
His valor and strength, for this people to use.
But the elders of Gilead, where once he did live,
To make him their chief this promise they give.

'Twas then he consented, and made a rash vow:
If the victory unto him, God would allow;
When unto his home, he again did return,
Whatsoever he met, for an offering he'd burn.
The children of Ammon he fought and defeated.
Alas, by his daughter, that he should be greeted.

'Twas then he repented, and bitterly wept,
Nevertheless, unto God, his rash vow was kept.
His dear only child, resigned to her fate,
Requested her father, two months only to wait.
With her companions she spent, the most of this time,
Who lamented the loss of this maiden sublime.

Jephthah's troubles it seems, were now only begun;
For the victories in battle, he so dearly had won,
Brought unto him jealousy, trouble, and strife;
Six years only he ruled, then ended his life.
For twenty-five years, there was peace in the land,
When these children again God's attention demand.
Notwithstanding, by him, so oft they were blest,
His laws, continually, by them were transgressed.
And so forty years subservient were they
To the Philistines, whom they were forced to obey.

Then Samson, when moved by the Lord he had been,
To deliver the Israelites, did strangely begin.
For, although a Danite, was this very strong man,
He married a Philistine, to consummate his plan.

With the strength of his hand, a lion he killed;
The carcass, with honey, by bees was well filled.

So he invited a company to a great feast,
And propounded a riddle, regarding the beast
He had killed—and the honey also.
Seven days, this riddle I'll give you to know,
Its import, if then, to me you declare,
A prize I will give in which you'll all share.

The forfeit is mine, if its meaning you miss.
The riddle he gave, was like unto this:
Out of the eater, came forth meat;
Out of the strong, came forth sweet.
His wife, with her friends, entered into a league,
The prize offered to gain, by fraud and intrigue.
Then Samson determined his wife he would leave,
And allow her no longer him thus to deceive.
But before his going from this people away,
Thirty of their number he managed to slay.

Then after a time, he concluded to go
Back again to his wife, some kindness to show.
But he learned that she now to another was wed;
And so in a contrary way he was led.
Procuring three hundred foxes, he together them tied,
And then a large cornfield, he took them beside;
With a fire brand attached, between every one,
All brightly burning, in the cornfield they run.

The corn, the olives, the vineyards were burned.
Then the Philistines' wrath on his father-in-law turned.

So by fire they consumed both father and daughter.
To be avenged, Samson great numbers did slaughter.
Then on his own way, from this people he went,
But to destroy him too the Philistines meant.
So went to his brethren, their story related:
And, with threats, this people they intimidated,
Until they consented they Samson would find,
And with very strong cords, also his limbs bind

When done, the Philistines feel much elated,
For Samson, they think, they have now subjugated.
But when the spirit of God fully over him came,
The Philistines, alas, were again put to shame.
His cords were broken, great numbers were slain
With the jaw bone of a beast, that before him had lain.

He brandished his weapon on the left and the right;
What few him escaped fled away in affright.
And now over Samson came a very great thirst;
So God caused water from the jaw bone to burst.
Samson, quenching his thirst, to the city of Gaza soon went,
Where he stopped at an Inn, and there the night spent.

But the Philistines here, for him lie in wait,
Surround entirely the city, and bar every gate.
The gates were thrown down by Samson with ease
Who to show his great strength, the iron gates seize.
The posts, the bars, he shoulders them all,
While the people, affrighted, backward then fall.

And now, very soon, Samson took for a wife;
A woman who proved the curse of his life.
Delilah, her name, of the Philistine race,
With morals imperfect, but a beautiful face.
Her own people bribe her to betray his great strength,
Three times he evaded, then told her, at length,
The cause of his wearing such very long hair;
By God 'twas ordained, his strength should be there.
Also from his head it should never be shorn;
As it grew every day, so let it be worn.

With his head in her lap she lulled him to sleep,
Then proceeded at once her promise to keep
With the people she held in much higher esteem
Than her husband, at least, so to us it doth seem:
His hair she braided and clipped from his head;
Then his eyes were put out and to Gaza he's led.

In the Philistines power, no pity had they,
For to work in the prison he was kept every day
But this people to honor their idols soon meet,
In the temple, and then, their sport to complete,
Sent for Samson, whose hair had been growing, alas,
Unnoticed, this people had let it all pass.
One room was supported by two pillars alone—
This fact, by Samson, before had been known—
And so he requested his attendant to rest—
By the side of the pillars, he thought would be best.
The pillars were broken, the temple o'erthrown,
With the strength of his arms, he did it alone.

Thus three thousand Philistines into eternity go:
While with them destroyed was Samson, also.

RUTH.

Now as judge over Israel, Eli prevailed;
'Twas a sorrowful time, for the crops had all failed;
And lest they should die, from want, and starvation,
Great numbers of the Israelites, resort to emigration.
So Elimelech of Bethlehem his family now take
To the land of Moab, a living to make;
His two sons married, all seemed to go well,
So ten years in Moab, they continue to dwell,
Then their fortunes reverse, these women bereft
Of their husbands, indeed, quite dependent are left.

Now Naomi, the mother, arose, and did say:
To my country and kindred I will hasten away.
So with her to go, Ruth and Orpha requested,
But Naomi, for some time, against this protested.
These maidens, although to her sons had been wed,
To serve heathen gods all their lives had been led.
But now Ruth determined her kindred to leave,
To the God of Naomi, she said, I will cleave.
And so they departed, leaving Orpha behind,
Who to stay with her parents at last seemed inclined.

When they Bethlehem reached, these women began
Their living to earn, and this was the plan:
Ruth desired Naomi at home to remain,
While she in the fields would glean for the grain
Which the reapers, in harvesting, leave loose on the
    ground,
The fields of Boaz were the first by her found.

This man, to Elimelech, was a relative near,
And to Ruth very kind, from the first did appear.
Unto Israel, by Moses, a law given had been,
A widow should marry her husband's next kin.
One nearer than Boaz there only remained,
So they were all called together, and the matter explained.

The person who was married to Ruth, it doth seem,
All the land of Elimelech now must redeem.
Boaz, being rich, could do this with ease;
So it fell to his lot, which did him much please.

The fruit of this union was a son, who became—
The father of Jesse, and Obed his name.
A descendant of Judah, as had been prophesied,
Unto Jesus of Nazareth he should be allied.

First Samuel.

Now Samuel, as judge, did Eli succeed;
In the succession of prophets he was first, as we read.
His father, Elcanah, until late in his life,
No child did possess, by Hannah his wife.
Two women, he married, Penninnah, the other—
Who of several children, already was mother.
For a son did Hannah most earnestly pray,
From the depths of her heart, did unto God say:
If the favor I ask, you'll grant unto me,
My son, to thy service, consecrated shall be.

Her petition was granted, remembered her vow;
As soon as the age of the child would allow,

She took him to the temple, a prophet to make,
Eli, the high priest, did charge of him take.
And because she gave Samuel unto the Lord,
Other children he gave her, as a reward.

Now young Samuel grew in God's favor each day,
But Eli's two sons did far from him stray,
Yet, had he rebuked them, as he certainly ought,
Perhaps unto God, they might have been brought.
But their idolatrous sins, now caused God to say:
Both Phinehas and Hophni shall die in one day.
Then the family of Eleazer, the priesthood will gain,
My temple in Shiloh thy sons would profane.

But the glory of Samuel did rapidly spread,
He had prophesied truly, for by God he was led.
And now the Philistine army, with hostile intent,
For the Israelite's sins, against them were sent.
The first battle fought, the Philistines gain,
And four thousand Israelites by them were slain.

Then Eli's two sons, and some others suggest
To set up the ark, its powers to test.
No reverence for the ark, had these men ever shown;
And so it was brought for protection alone.
For this added sin, in the next battle fought,
Great havoc among them the Philistines wrought.

Thirty thousand were slain, the rest driven away,
Both Phinehas and Hophni were killed in the fray.
The ark by the enemy, being captured also,
A messenger was sent, at once, to Shiloh.

'Twas there, from the temple, the ark had been brought,
The news concerned Eli, the most, it was thought.

The death of his sons, with composure he heard,
But the loss of the ark, so deeply him stirred,
That he fell from his seat and immediately died;
He'd been watching it seems, out by the way side.
On the same fatal day did Phinehas' wife
For her infant son Ichabod, yield up her life.

The ark was now carried to a temple in Ashdod;
And set up beside the Philistine's god.
This idol, was made part fish and part man,
And to tumble and fall it immediately began.
But the Philistines retained the ark just the same;
And so a necessity unto God it became,
A terrible plague among them to send —
Great numbers in torture their lives did thus end.
While myriads of mice sprang out of the earth,
Which of all vegetation caused a great dearth.

The Philistines alarmed, sent the ark here and there,
But to keep it, at last, no city did dare.
For destruction was certain, wherever it went,
So they decided to Israel it now must be sent.
And two kine being tied before a new cart,
With the ark, and some offerings, thus they did start.

If the kine, without driving, to the Israelites go,
The cause of their trouble was the ark, they will know.
To a village in Judah the kine went straight way:
So the Israelites rejoiced, did the ark then convey

To a stone in the field; and some looking therein,
Immediately died for committing the sin.

The kine and the cart for an offering were burned,
The Philistines then to their own homes returned
Satisfied that the ark was in the right place,
And that it was only intended for the Israelite race.
Now Eleazer was sanctified, the ark placed in his care,
While to worship God only, the Israelites prepare.

Entreated by Samuel, the false gods were destroyed,
And in praying to Jehovah they were oft'times employed.
For this purpose, at Mizpeh, they had one day collected;
The Philistines, hearing they were there unprotected,
Mustered their forces, and in battle array,
Intended the Israelites to capture and slay.

But Samuel, with prayer, did a sacrifice make,
And, in answer, God sent a terrific earthquake,
Which destroyed them in part, the rest frightened away;
So the Israelites pursued them and carried the day.
Then Samuel set a stone, and Ebenezer it named,
Hitherto hath God helped us, by him was proclaimed.

Some lands of the Hebrews the Philistines possessed
'Twas taken by them in some previous conquest—
This Samuel recovered, and thus ended the strife
Between these two nations, during his life.
His home was at Ramah, his altar also,
But as judge over Israel to many cities must go.

When feeble with age, that a rest he might take,
His sons Joel and Abiah, of them judges did make.
But they judgment perverted, and unto Israel bring
Disaster and ruin, until they beg for a king.

Unto Samuel they come, with this urgent request,
Who was not only disturbed but greatly distressed.
God said unto Samuel: Be thou of good cheer,
For this wickedness, Israel shall pay very dear.
So long I have kept them from danger protected,
To be forsaken, forgotten, and also rejected.
Then grant them their wish, but first to them state,
By choosing a king what must be their fate.

In the city of Gibeah was a Benjaminite, Saul,
A choice young man, likewise very tall.
He came unto Ramah, the prophet to see—
God had said unto Samuel, I'll send him to thee.
So Samuel was watching, and when he drew near,
God immediately said, the king doth appear.

Then, as soon as Saul's business he had disclosed,
To stay over night was by Samuel proposed.
So he waited till morning, and before he departed,
The secret to Saul was by Samuel imparted.
Then together they went to the city outside,
Where alone, on Saul's head, the oil was applied.
Thus as king over Israel, was Saul there anointed,
But, ere leaving him, Samuel still farther appointed,
You shall go to Gilgal, I will meet with you there;
For the work you're intended, you then shall prepare.

A company of prophets you will meet on the way,
And then, if the spirit of God you obey,

A true prophet among them, at once you will be,
While the people shall wonder your glory to see.

Soon the Israelites meet their king to proclaim,
But no answer is given, when they call out his name;
Saul shrank from appearing, so modest was he;
But when he was brought where the people could see,
So high above all he carried his head,
God save the king, was by every one said.

Now Samuel wrote out some laws to obey,
And put them in the sanctuary safely away.
Then they went to their homes, but there was trouble ahead,
For the sons of Belial were by jealousy led.
Two years passed by, and then the Philistines began
An invasion in Israel to artfully plan.
But Saul had an army of three thousand at hand;
Jonathan his son, helped him them to command.

A small army of spies, first the Philistines sent out,
Not many are slain, but they're soon put to rout.
Then a large army came; no treaty would make,
Except the right eye of each person they take.
The people of the city where the invasion was made
Begged them wait a few days, while the matter is weighed;
Then send for king Saul, who attacked them at night,
Many thousands are slain, the rest put to flight.

This victory gained, by some 'twas suggested,
To slay every one who against Saul had protested,

But the king said nay, that never would do;
'Twas not I, but God, that carried us through.
Then they go to Gilgal, and there Saul reordain,
For the desire is now mutual, as king he should reign.

Then Samuel his judgeship resigned, and in love
Bade them look unto God, all others above.
Your request for a king did him seriously grieve;
That this you may know and fully believe;
I will call upon him this moment to send—
A storm, that shall lightning and thunder attend.

It came with such violence, the people drew near
To Samuel, who assured them they had nothing to fear;
For if your allegiance unto God you will give;
He will guide and protect you, as long as you live.
Now a king you have chosen, be loyal and true
For your love and obedience is unto him due.

The Philistines recovering from their last conflict and rout,
In battle array were now skirmishing about,
Jonathan and his armor bearer attacked them alone
His great faith in God, in this manner was shown.

When I challenge a battle, if they ask me to wait,
'Tis prophetic, most surely, that defeat is my fate;
But if to come up at once they boldly should cry,
For the victory then on God I'll rely.

Now, as they bade him to come, so Jonathan went;
God a terrible earthquake to help him then sent.

While the Philistines, helpless, trembled in fear;
Saul, seeing the battle, with reinforcements drew near.
Then to the Israelites again the victory was given,
And out of their country the Philistines driven.

Saul, as a commander, was judicious and brave,
So a message from God, Samuel unto him gave:
The Amalekites now must be utterly exterminated,
For the outrages on the Hebrews, in the wilderness perpetrated.
Their women, their children, and possessions spare not,
That the name of Amalek shall be only a blot.

Saul gathered his forces together and then,
He numbered four hundred and thirty thousand men.
All artful devices by him were emyloyed,
Until the Amalekites were entirely destroyed.
But the king, Saul unwisely decided to spare;
The soldiers also of the spoils saved a share.

Saul reported to Samuel the victory gained,
But God had previously unto Samuel explained
How Saul had saved the Amalekite king,
Which on himself ruin most surely would bring.
So Samuel rebuked him, and thus prophesied:
Since God's laws you've transgressed and him you've defied,
As he punished your fathers, so with you it will be —
Another king over Israel, you will very soon see.

Saul entreated Samuel the spoils now to take
As a sacrifice to God, a burnt offering make;

Also with the king to do as he please;
God's wrath in this way he thought to appease.
But Samuel, through God, was prompted to say,
Far better than sacrifice is it to obey.

Saul his transgressions did now bitterly repent,
So to worship the Lord he with Samuel went.
And then, God's commands to further fulfill,
The Amalekite king, Samuel decided to kill.
Then he parted with Saul, to meet nevermore,
But his wilful disobedience he did greatly deplore.

Until God at length bade him his grief to restrain,
For another king over Israel he now must ordain.
To the house of Jesse, was Samuel directed,
For one of his sons, as king, was elected.
But Samuel fearing that Saul might him slay;
Was instructed by God to proceed in this way.

To the house of Jesse, in Bethlehem, take
A heifer, of which a sacrifice make.
Call the family together, and then I'll appoint
The one I desire, as king you'll anoint.
But Samuel was puzzled, for each one selected,
Instead of accepting, God immediately rejected.

And then unto Jesse did Samuel draw near,
Appealed to him thus, are your children all here?
He answered, another, the youngest of all,
Is tending the sheep. Said Samuel, him call.
'Twas David, God chose him, not for his size,
But for purity of heart—a far greater prize.
Although anointed as king, it still was unknown—
Save unto his family and Samuel alone.

Now Saul, being troubled, sent his servants to find
A harper, whose music would comfort his mind.
They were directed to David, the grandson of Ruth,
A skillful performer, also a brave youth.
So well he succeeded in soothing Saul's mind,
To keep him awhile was this great man inclined.

But soon his attention was drawn far away,
For the Philistines again, in battle array,
Have invaded the country, and a champion great
Has challenged a combat, to determine their fate.
His name was Goliath, a giant so tall,
The sight of him even, did the strongest appall.

Now David at home, to the camp he was sent,
To inquire for his brothers, who as soldiers there went;
The giant he saw, the challenge he heard,
But the fear of the soldiers seemed to David absurd,
Who, determined to meet him, but in the Lord's name;
It was not for glory, self honor, nor fame.

His brothers derided, and Saul expressed fear;
But David the calmest of all did appear.
He assured them Jehovah would for him now care,
Who had saved him from a lion and the paw of a bear.
So when he went forth, to meet the giant, he took—
His staff, a sling, and five stones from the brook.
Although with Saul's weapons he had first been supplied,
At last upon God, and his own, he relied.

When Goliath saw David, in disdain he cried out,
For that he'd destroy him he had not a doubt.
Now David prepared his sling with a stone,
Then, directed by God, at the giant 'twas thrown,
And between his two eyes it entered his brain;
Thus proving God's power, for Goliath was slain.

With the giant's own sword David cut off his head,
While the Philistines, in terror, precipitately fled.
But the Israelites now them boldly pursued;
Thirty thousand were killed, thus the Philistines subdued.
At Jerusalem, the head of Goliath was shown,
For such a valorous deed was never before known.
Even Saul, with David, was perfectly delighted,
And to remain in his home for a time him invited;
Thus Jonathan and David as brothers became,
'Twas a union of hearts, not simply a name.

Now David, so popular, his praises were chanted,
Which irritated Saul, who was continually haunted
By the prophecy of Samuel; for too well he knew,
Inspired by God, his prophecies were true.
At length of David so jealous Saul grew,
A javelin, with violence, at him he threw.

But David escaped, and, to lull his suspicion,
Over an army of a thousand Saul gave him commission.
The Philistines, in battle, will doubtless him slay;
He thought to dispose of David this way.
And so while secretly scheming for his life,
He promised his daughter should be David's wife.

The eldest, Merab, was the first he did mention,
But, after a time, he changed his intention:
And said, if one hundred Philistines you'll slaughter,
I'll give you Michal, my next oldest daughter.

For Merab to another he had given away;
And now he has planned a second delay,
As he did not intend either promise to fulfil,
For the Philistines, he expected, would David easily kill.
But David soon brought the proof unto Saul,
That two hundred Philistines did by his hand fall.

That the Lord was with David Saul now plainly saw,
So his promise he dare not, this time to withdraw.
And that Michal loved David he also could see;
But his enemy still he continued to be.
For, soon after the marriage, did Saul openly say,
Now David shall die without farther delay.
But Jonathan, with Saul, so earnestly pleaded,
To restore him to favor for a while he succeeded.
And so, between Saul and David peace reigned,
Until in a battle the victory was gained
By David, whom all the people loved well,
And therefore were pleased his praises to tell.

Saul in anger one day, when David was near,
Again attempted his life by throwing his spear.
The spear he escaped, but must have soon lost his life,
Had it not been for Michal, his true, loving wife.
Saul's servants that night, to David kept near,
For to kill him, was ordered, when he should appear.

But his wife, through the window, slyly letting him down,
Her father deceived, until he was out of the town.

His steps unto Ramah were immediately directed,
For by Samuel, he felt, he would now be protected.
No trouble had he in Samuel's home reaching,
And when he arrived, a school of prophets he was teaching.
Saul, hearing he was there, some officers sent,
To capture and arrest him, was now their intent;
But seeing the prophets, their minds were diverted,
So they tarried awhile, and themselves were converted.
Then Saul started out, and when to Ramah he came,
Lo, the Spirit of God came upon him the same.

Now Saul, to be friendly to David doth appear;
But for his sincerity, David and Jonathan both fear.
So Jonathan bade David himself to secrete,
While he at a feast with his father would meet,
By resorting to a ruse, his intentions he'd learn;
With the information gained, then to David return.

And now again David owed his life to this friend;
Who at the risk of his *own*, determined him to defend.
As Jonathan explained, David's absence, from the feast,
Each moment Saul's anger by it was increased,
Until he at last threw his spear at his son,
As before unto David he had several times done.

Jonathan escaped, but with a sorrowful heart,
For he knew he and David most surely must part.
He met him, and told him his story all through,
Then they affectionately bade each other adieu.
Now David, for safety, left this city behind,
To visit the high priest, he first was inclined.
His visit was short, but some food he procured,
And the sword of Goliath he also secured.

In the city of Gath, he next stopped to rest,
But the Philistines soon his identity guessed.
So then, cunningly, madness was by him feigned:
Otherwise, his freedom he would never have gained.

And now in no place dare he lay down his head,
So to hide in the caves at last he is led,
Where about four hundred men as leader him chose,
Brave men, also loyal, so his courage arose.
They were joined by a prophet, who advised them
    to go
Into the forests of Hareth, their Valor there show.

But David, sad news, was soon destined to hear,
For at the camp in the forest one day did appear
Abiathar, who unto the high priest was son;
In his family, alas, he was now all the one.
By Saul's order the priests had been put to an end;
When he heard that Ahimelech did David befriend.
This sad news David heard, with a sorrowful heart,
So he said to Abiathar, from me do not depart;
The life of your father for me has been taken;
I will see that his son shall not be forsaken.

And now we read David by Saul was constantly
 pursued,
But that directed by God, he did him some way
 elude.
At one time a mountain alone them separated;
But that Saul should come nearer it was not predes-
 tinated.
For the Philistines had invaded his country he
 learned,
And thus his attention was suddenly turned.

But the invaders repelled, with three thousand men,
His search for David is then taken up again.
To the wilderness of Engedi he tracked him at last;
His hiding place often Saul closely had passed.
One day all alone while sleeping in a cave,
Doth David the life of his enemy save.

His followers would have killed him, but David said
 nay,
I will cut off his skirt then send him away.
But ere he permitted King Saul to depart,
He assured him that love alone reigned in his heart.
David's righteouness now by Saul was confessed,
And for sparing his life, he also him blessed.
Then, too, he acknowledge, unto him it was plain,
As Israel's king one day he would reign.

Impulsive as ever, he bade David adieu,
With affection that seemed both fervent and true.
But David well knowing his changeable mind,
To put himself in his power was in no way inclined.

Now the death of Samuel did all Israel lament;
He was buried at Ramah, where his last years were spent.
This affliction did David most deeply affect,
For Samuel he held in the highest respect.

An exile from home, no settled habitation;
Deplorable indeed, now seemed his situation.
Although penitent was Saul, when they last separated,
A renewal of his anger, was by David anticipated.
And so from Engedi, to Paran, he moved;
An adventurous change, as it afterward proved.

A man of great wealth, named Nabal, lived there,
David tended his flocks, for a very small share.
But this avaricious man was false in his dealing,
So between him and David arose a bitter feeling.
Which had it not been for Nabal's good wife,
Might have led to a battle, and the taking of life.

For six hundred men had David at hand,
Who were ready to obey his slightest command.
With four hundred he had started, in battle array,
When Nabal's wife Abigail, he met on the way.
Who well knew that David, by Nabal was wronged,
So the provisions she brought which to him then belonged.

And there the matter was dropped, for Abigail's sake,
But a lasting impression, her kindness did make,
For very soon after, Nabal departed this life,
And Abigail became, unto David, a wife.

Another husband had Michal, and David two wives,
Thus the wickedness of Saul affected both of their lives.

And now when of David's adventures Saul heard,
His bosom again was by jealousy stirred.
And again, when seeking his life, is his own
Into the hands of David, providentially thrown.
Who would not permit that harm should befall,
The anointed of the Lord, and so he spared Saul.

But unto his conscience he made an appeal,
Which softened his heart, in a way that seemed real;
But David dare not this capricious man trust,
So to change his locality he felt, that he must.
And now through fear, he is led into sin,
In the city of Gath, where before he had been.
He went to the king and sought his protection,
While agreeing to act, now under his direction.
With his six hundred men, therefore, he was sent,
To fight his *own* people, and accordingly went.

But instead of harming, in any way, the Israelites,
He utterly destroyed the people of the Geshurites:
Their cattle, and camels, to the king he then brought;
That they were taken from the Israelites, the Philistines thought,
Now the Philistine king, a great army collected,
For to destroy the Israelites, was by him projected;
And so thinking David was with them allied,
Again for assistance, unto him he applied.

He was obliged to consent, for he dare not object;
Lest the deceit he had practiced they now would detect.

Saul viewing the army, fled away terrified,
To the witch of Endor, to whom he applied
For direction; he begged she would Samuel call;
Immediately the witch, cried out, thou art Saul.
Of witches, this one did now only remain,
For the rest, by Saul's orders, before had been slain.
So fearing a snare for her destruction was laid,
To reveal what she saw, she sought to evade;
Nor would she consent, to Samuel call,
Until her protection was sworn to by Saul.

Then in connection with what had been prophesied,
By Samuel to Saul sometime ere he died,
Through this woman, he now did furthermore say,
The Philistines in the battle shall carry the day.
But the prediction which caused him far greater sorrow,
Was that himself and three sons should die on the morrow.
The battle was fought, the prediction came true:
For Saul and his sons by swords were pierced through.

But David and his men, had no part in the affray:
For, by the Philistines' wishes, they were ordered away.
And so very gladly to their homes they returned,
To find by the Amalekites they had been burned,

Their wives, and their children, taken as captives
    away;
To consult the high priest, they did only delay.
Then following after, their encampment discovered;
Through the aid of an Egyptian, their possessions
    recovered.

SECOND SAMUEL.

When they returned to the camp, they heard the sad
    news,
How badly defeated had been the Hebrews.
Also that King Saul, and his three sons, were slain;
David's sorrow no longer he then could restrain.
'Twas an Amalekite soldier, who the message them
    brought,
And to gain the full particulars, David then sought.
So he learned that this man, Saul to obey,
When certain of death, with the sword did him slay.
The truth of his message more plainly to show,
Saul's bracelets, and crown, he delivered also.

As God's anointed, for Saul, did David now weep,
But his sorrow for Jonathan was intensely deep;
He loved him in life, he mourned for him, dead,
His love too for me, was most wonderful, he said.
The Philistines continuing victorious, now possessed—
All the land on the side of the Jordan called west.
So the Israelites were forced the east side to take;
And at Hebron a king of David they make.

But Abner, Saul's general, of David was jealous,
So to him supersede, he became very zealous.

And a nominal king he makes of Saul's son;
Ishbosheth, surviving, is there no other one.
But the house of Judah followed David alone;
Their aversion to Ishbosheth, plainly was shown.
And so in civil wars, they engage for five years,
With varying results, so it plainly appears,
As David's general Joab, his nephew, arose,
And Abner, for Ishbosheth, did him oppose.

Now the power of David did gradually increase,
For the reign of Ishbosheth very soon was to cease.
So Abner, realizing how matters would end,
Overtures unto David thought best to send.
He proffered his friendship and with it his aid,
So accordingly David, this proposition made:

Six sons had he now, every one were half brothers,
'Tis plain to be seen they had all different mothers;
But David his first wife, now also desired,
So to restore unto him Michal, of Abner required:
To accomplish his desire, Abner readily consented;
And Michal to David ere long was presented.

Now a visit to David was by Abner projected;
Twenty men as a guard, his person protected.
By David he was treated so kindly and fair,
He promised the wrongs he had done to repair.
With this resolution his homeward way wending,
No presentiment had he, of the danger impending.

But Joab of his visit, soon chancing to learn,
In David's name immediately requests he'll return.

The messenger sent was instructed to say,
There was business of importance the king dare not
    delay.
Abner immediately returned and was met at the gate
By Joab, who asked him a moment to wait;
Then he and his brother, Abishai, did slay
Abner, in this wicked and treacherous way.
In committing the deed they themselves justified,
Because Asahel, their brother, by Abner's hand died.

But David would not these brothers excuse,
And publicly stated to the people his views.
The deed he condemned, then called on the Lord,
According to their wickedness, them to reward.
At the burial of Abner, David followed the bier,
And thus to the people his grief seemed sincere.

When Ishbosheth heard that Abner was dead,
In weakness he often would take to his bed,
For his power he depended on Abner alone;
As his league with David he never had known.
But not long was he left to mourn for the dead;
For he was murdered by traitors, who cut off his head,
Then presented it to David, his favor to gain,
But instead, he ordered them both to be slain.

And now all Israel, with David delighted,
To make him their king, were perfectly united.
His army, thirty thousand or more now contained;
With it over Jerusalem a victory was gained.
But before 'twas accomplished, some hard fighting
    was done,
And in the battle great honors, by Joab, were won.

Now in repairing the city, some time was employed
As the battle its beauty had greatly destroyed.
A wall David caused to be built all around,
When a more compact city there could not be found.
The taking of Jerusalem was a very great thing;
This triumph to David great honors doth bring.

The most powerful potentate the world did then know,
Sent unto him presents, his friendship to show.
This great king over Tyre, called Hiram, by name,
His alliance with David when well known it became,
So strengthened his power, all nations then fear,
An enemy unto him to openly appear.

But his prosperity led him into folly and sin—
For although a polygamist he some time had been—
'Twas a practice then general and no doubt thought right:
But to establish a harem was a sin in God's sight.
This David did do, but was afterwards shown,
That we surely must reap the same as we've sown.
His manner of living contempt on him brought,
Thus to subdue him with ease the Philistines thought;
But when they drew near, Jerusalem to take,
Confession to Jehovah David did make;
So notwithstanding twice, they attempt an attack,
Each time God assisted him in driving them back.

His gratitude to Jehovah he now wished to prove,
So the ark to Jerusalem said he would move;
But not until God had himself manifested,
Was the ark in Jerusalem finally rested.

For while on the way it was by the cart shaken,
When Uzzah had scarcely hold of it taken
Before he was stricken down perfectly dead;
For no person should touch it but a priest, had God said.

And although a number were in the procession,
David fearing in some way another transgression,
Left the ark with Obededom, a God-fearing man
Three months, when to move it again he began.
On the shoulders of priests, this time it was borne,
And by David we read a linen ephod was worn,
Sacrifices of oxen and fatlings were made,
Also musical instruments were joyously played.

Michal witnessing David's exuberant joy,
Instead of rejoicing, this did her annoy.
But David assured her, it was all for the Lord;
His love, and approval, would him amply reward.
David's heart with gratitude to God being filled,
A repository for the ark, he desired to build.
For instruction on Nathan, the prophet, he depended,
By whom this new project was highly commended.

But God deemed the work, as yet, premature,
And bade David first his kingdom secure,
Which, after his death, should be ruled by his son;
Also the work he had planned by him should be done.
Then a war of subjugation David immediately began,
Joab over his army being placed as first man.

Nearly all of Palestine, was by David subjugated:
And a share of the spoils unto God dedicated.

Now after Saul's family, David was led to inquire,
For to do them a kindness was his earnest desire.
One son had Jonathan then living he learned;
So his dear friend's kindness could now be returned.
Saul's land to his grandson, David restored,
Also with his own family he took him to board.

But soon he is forced to call out his men,
To take up their arms in battle again,
For when the king of Ammon death did remove,
Then David, desiring his true friendship to prove,
Condoling messages sent unto his son—
And although 'twas sincerely and properly done,
The young king's brothers, by false insinuations,
Put an end forever to all friendly relations.

And caused a battle, also, to be fought,
Which unto the Ammonites complete ruin brought.
And we read that David during this strife,
Committed the greatest sin of his life:
The armor-bearer of Joab, a warrior of fame,
Had a beautiful wife, Bathsheba by name,
And David now conceived a most heinous plan
To rid himself entirely of this valorous man.

By ordering Joab in the next battle fought,
To the fore front of the army this man must be brought.
Then only with him a short time to remain,
That he by the enemy could be easily slain.

Thus Uriah was forced to give up his life,
And David then made of Bathsheba a wife.

Now God did Nathan the prophet, thus move,
To go unto David, and for this sin him reprove.
And this righteous man dare not God disobey;
So to David he went with a parable straightway,
Wherein the evildoer, not as guilty as he,
David his fault most plainly could see.
And then Nathan, the prophet, the parable applied;
Prophesying his future punishment beside.

When the predictions of Nathan David had heard,
His conscience with remorse and anguish was stirred;
And now unto God he most fervently prayed
That the judgments predicted by his hand might be stayed.
Who promised to preserve his kingdom and life,
But the son now born unto Bathsheba his wife,
He declared, as Nathan did the same prophesy,
Should be stricken with disease and very soon die.

The child's illness caused David uncontrollable grief,
But, when dead, the people, seeing his seeming relief,
Ventured to inquire the cause of his change,
His answer, no doubt, to some did seem strange.
While the child lived, knowing God to be gracious,
I hoped that my prayers might be efficacious.

But now I'll not murmur, for 'twas God's decree—
I shall go unto him, he'll return not to me.

'Twas pleasing to God, who on David now smiled,
And gave unto Bathsheba another male child,
Whom we shall call Solomon, hereafter, by name,
And for him was predicted a life of great fame.
But what was by far, the most wonderful thing;
That from his descendants Messiah should spring.

After Solomon's birth, a cruel battle was fought,
Which under subjection, the Ammonites brought.
The hottest of the battle by David was led;
When the king's crown was taken and set on his head,
Which being very valuable, was held in high estimate,
Of gold and precious stones, a talent its weight.

But now David's children, absorb his attention,
Amnon, Absalom, and Tamar, these now we shall mention.
Amnon, for Tamar, an unholy passion conceived;
For the indulgence of which Tamar sorely was grieved.
So she imparted to Absalom the cause of her grief,
Who, with comforting words, sought his sister's relief;
And although his anger, controlled for her sake,
Resolved, nevertheless, the life of Amnon to take.

So he invited his brothers all with him to dine,
And his servants slew Amnon while merry with wine.
The news was carried to David this way:
Absalom, his brothers, did every one slay.

David's sons delaying their homeward return;
Sometime had elapsed, ere the truth he did learn;
And although Amnon was a well beloved child,
That he was the only, doubtless him some reconciled.

To inquire after Absalom, soon David was led,
Who to the King of Geshur, his grandfather, had fled.
Three years from his home, did he an exile remain,
When to send for him by Joab, David was fain.
But when he returned, by his father's decree,
Two years passed by ere his face he did see.

For his father's coldness was Absalom oppressed;
Accordingly of Joab he made this request,
Wilt thou go to my father, and him pacify?
If not, 'twere far better that now I should die
So then David, by Joab, being implored,
His favor to Absalom, immediately restored,
Who not long to his father, a true friend remained;
And therefore his sorrow must have been feigned.

To be king over Israel is now his ambition,
And so, by intrigue, he gains the position;
A large army he raised, and to Jerusalem went,
To take both the city and his father was meant.
But David, being warned, had hastened away,
With six hundred followers in the wilderness to stay.

And here his life must have been sacrificed,
Of his impending danger had he not been apprised.
Also the same friend, his design to perfect,
In Absalom's plan pointed out a defect.

Although the first plan, by a friend was conceived,
The cunning device of the latter was believed,
And instead of pursuing his father straightway,
To be reinforced, for some time did delay;
In the meantime, David, somewhat unexpected,
Was by a large army, sustained and protected.

Although as king over Israel, Absalom did reign
His continual fear he was unable to restrain,
For while David lived, he knew not what hour
Dethroned he should be, and deprived of all power.
So he gathered his forces, and marched with them away,
Hoping in the battle his father to slay.

Now David loved Absalom, and begged in the strife,
No one would attempt to deprive him of life.
But the battle was fought, and Absalom slain,
David's army, also, did the victory gain.
Although Absalom by Joab was purposely killed,
It would seem 'twas destiny being fulfilled:
For in the branches of an oak tree was Absalom caught,
And there remained hanging until Joab was brought,
Who hesitated not, in well doing his part,
And thrust three javelins into his heart.

Then David cried out, when hearing 'twas done,
Would God I had died for thee, Absalom, my son;
In his grief he neglected his troops to commend,
Until Joab the evils of his course did portend,
And threatened his influence against him to use,
Unless he accorded to the people their dues.

In this way he's induced to sit in the gate,
The coming of the soldiers there to await.

Aroused from his melancholy, he sees very plain,
No longer in seclusion must he remain
And now Absalom dead, the people make known
Their desire for David to occupy the throne,
While several, with penitent spirits, implore
His forgiveness and love to them he'll restore.
Accordingly David full pardon proclaimed,
Unto each and to all who had him defamed.

The Judahites for David now being very zealous,
This caused the Benjaminites to be angry and jealous;
So one of their number, Sheba by name,
Saw fit at this time a war to proclaim,
Which did David grieve, but there was only one way
To crush the revolt, and without any delay.

So to muster his forces in this way he began :
By appointing Amasa to act as head man ;
A commander he'd been, during Absalom's reign,
David thought it discreet he should continue the same.
To suppress the rebellion he accordingly went,
But David, uneasy, soon Joab, too, sent,
Who acting unto Amasa a traitorous part,
Seemed friendly, while piercing with a dagger his heart.

Then Joab, as leader, did Sheba pursue,
In a city near Jordan, they came in full view
Of his army, which their danger now fully realize,
And to save their own lives they act in this wise:

Through a sage woman, with Joab, a treaty was made,
For the head of Sheba, the conflict was stayed.

With the Philistines now soon follows a strife,
In which king David came near losing his life.
'Twas after the battle, the Philistines defeated,
David wishing to rest, so had himself seated,
When a giant rushed up, with a huge spear,
As large as Goliath's, or if not very near.

But the brother of Joab, Abishai by name,
To the assistance of David immediately came;
The giant was slain, and now David retired
From battles, hereafter, as his people desired.
Three victories more, the Israelites gain;
Each time, a giant, single-handed was slain.

Now David had peace for a considerable time,
And wrote many songs, most truly sublime.
The Psalms, at this period nearly all were conceived,
If the opinion of Josephus may by us be believed.
But it seems after a time, his uneasy mind,
Tempted by Satan, some evil doth find.

So he forces Joab, who commander is still,
To number the people against his own will.
The labor to accomplish, occupied several men,
Time amounting to months, we find nearly ten.
Thirteen hundred thousand, was the number all told,
The census takers had, as soldiers enrolled.

But a dream unto David, God having sent,
Causes him now to most sincerely repent.

And in answer to prayer, through a prophet God spake,
Your choice in three things I'll allow you to take.
Three months from enemies constantly flee,
Seven years famine, or days of pestilence three.

David was now placed in a terrible strait,
But he knew God's mercies, to be very great;
The pestilence chosen, seventy thousand were killed,
And then God's heart, with compassion was filled.
For David an altar had unto him made,
And, by his entreaties, the plague was now stayed.

FIRST KINGS.

And now David's son, Adonijah, we read,
Desired as king his father to succeed.
So with Abiathar, the priest, and Joab conferred,
By whom his desires were approvingly heard.
But Solomon as king had David designated;
So Nathan, the prophet, to Bathsheba related
All about the conspiracy, and told her, also,
That she unto David must immediately go.

The interests of Solomon, her son, to secure,
So she and Nathan did from David procure
An order for Solomon's anointing, straightway;
He shall sit on my throne, said David, this day,
When proclaimed as king, the people all shout—
Thus proving their joy without any doubt.

Adonijah at this time was guests entertaining—
As a nominal king for a while he'd been reigning;

But fearing that Solomon would him now slay,
For safety he fled some distance away.
But Solomon assured him no harm should be done
If he, in the future, all evil would shun.

And now David having but a short time to live,
Calls his people together, his last charge to give.
The plan of the temple, which he once thought to build,
He left with Solomon, as by God had been willed.
And told him forever to walk in God's ways;
For thus he would prosper all of his days.
Forty years as a king, had David then reigned,
And that now he should rest by God was ordained.
He was buried at Jerusalem, the city called his own;
Great respect for his memory by his people was shown.
Now God in a dream, of Solomon inquired,
Of all earthly blessings, what most he desired.
First his weakness unto God he humbly confessed,
And with an understanding heart, then asked to be blest.
Solomon's spirit was so pleasing, in the sight of the Lord,
That he promised great wisdom should be his reward.
Also honor and riches, said he, too, I will give;
And if me you'll obey many years you shall live.
But Adonijah still hopes, his fortune to retrieve,
And an infamous project, he now doth conceive.
Not a very long time before David died,
To Abishag the Shunammite he was allied.

Adonijah's idea was this woman to wed,
Then the crown, he surmised, would be placed on
 his head.
Accordingly to Bathsheba, Solomon's mother he
 went,
And begged her obtain of the king his consent.
Now although Bathsheba was by Adonijah deceived,
Solomon at once his iniquity perceived,
And ordered Benaiah, his half brother, to slay;
Then unto Abiathar did furthermore say;
Thou art worthy of death, but thou didst the ark bear;
And so for a time I will thy life spare.

Joab well knowing the wrongs he had done,
In King David's time, and now to his son,
For safety, unto the sanctuary fled;
And remained, till the guard cut off his head.
For when Solomon ordered him brought to his trial,
The messenger reported, his absolute denial
Of leaving the place, which his presence polluted,
And so he was there by Benaiah executed.

Who was then appointed, by Solomon as head,
In the army, where once Joab had led.
And likewise Zadok, in Abiathar's stead,
High priest should be, so Solomon said.
And now the obedience of Shimei to prove,
He ordered from Jerusalem never to move;
For David we find, warned Solomon of this man,
And preceding his death placed him under a ban.

Shimei took an oath, in Jerusalem to remain,
Otherwise the decree, that he should be slain.

His oath he kept until three years had passed by,
And then, being ignored, this man had to die.
The great wisdom of Solomon to all is now shown;
Two mothers professed the same child to own.
To divide the child and make of it two,
Solomon said, now, I can no other way do.

Slay not my son, the real mother cried,
But the other insisted that he should it divide.
The true mother love so forcibly expressed,
Solomon considered as an indubitable test.
And so was the child restored to its mother,
While publicly condemned was the wickedness of
    the other.

That Solomon was endowed with a divine mind,
All Israel to believe, now seemed inclined.
Indeed, his wisdom did greatly exceed
The men of all nations, in the Bible we read;
Also of this assertion we have a credible token,
As three thousand proverbs were by him spoken:
Beside, one thousand and five songs he composed,
At different times, before his life closed.

To begin the temple now was Solomon constrained;
That this work should be his, he knew was ordained.
King Hiram of Tyre, had to him overtures made;
So in this great undertaking he solicited his aid.
The timber to Joppa, by Hiram was sent,
And Solomon's servants, there, after it went.
The outside of the temple of hewed stone was made,
The inside was cedar with gold overlaid.

Precious stones were added, until the effect was sublime.
The building of the temple exhausted seven years' time.

In Mount Moriah at Jerusalem, it was located;
The identical spot by God designated
For Abraham, of Isaac, a sacrifice to make;
A most fitting place, if only for his sake.
The temple completed, was then dedicated,
Both king and people in the ceremonies participated.
The priests and the Levites did the ark bear
To the Holy of Holies, and rested it there.

This place in the temple, for the ark had been made,
Two cherubim placed there, with gold overlaid.
Under their wide spreading wings and behind the Holy veil,
No evil-minded person the ark could assail.
The Levites were clad in garments of white,
And in a sacred chorus their voices unite,
The joyful refrain, was an expression of love
To God, who was merciful all others above.
In the midst of their praises a thick cloud doth appear,
Which assures them that God is unto them near.

Now Solomon before the congregation did kneel,
And made unto God a most solemn appeal.
Following which, from Heaven, was sent down a fire;
To manifest his glory, God doth seemingly desire.
Then the king and his people, sacrifices made,
While the Levites and priests on instruments played.

And now a fourteen days feast, after which the
  people depart,
For the goodness of Jehovah glad and merry in
  heart.

The Lord's house completed, now Solomon began
A palace for himself more leisurely to plan;
'Twas a magnificent structure, when finished at last,
And by no building but the Temple was it surpassed.
In the construction of the palace, so it appears,
The whole time employed was just thirteen years

Now above all other kings, was Solomon noted,
Indeed, his great wisdom, was by all nations quoted.
To a king's daughter in Egypt, some time he'd been
  wed,
Which connection, no doubt, somewhat his fame
  spread.
Of this wonderful king, the queen of Sheba heard
  with the rest,
And so, with hard questions, came his wisdom to
  test;
But, when his wisdom and wealth, the queen did
  behold,
She acknowledged the half had never been told.
Costly presents were exchanged, and then she
  returned,
To tell of the wonderful things she had learned.

Solomon's wealth increased, until silver became,
In abundance as stones, even the same.
His throne was ivory, with gold overlaid;
His drinking vessels, also, of the same metal made.

Aside from his riches, which were indeed very great.
The Canaanites all, were to him subjugate.
Surely his blessings, now, seemed beyond measure,
But at last he is led to incur God's displeasure.

Many women he loved from idolatrous nations,
And with them he entered into connubial relations,
Notwithstanding that God, had unto Israel said,
With no other nation thy people shall wed.
For he knew if to idolaters they were allied,
Jehovah by them would then be denied.

Three hundred concubines and seven hundred wives.
Solomon sought, to make happy their lives.

So he worshiped their idols, which did him deprave,
And in an inglorious manner he was brought to his grave.
Then although the kingdom was not taken away,
For king David's sake, during Solomon's day,
His son to succeed him, God did not ordain;
For only over two tribes was he permitted to reign.

And now Solomon's conduct, many enemies him bring,
First Hadad subdued Syria, and reigned there as king,
Then Israel he invaded, and, with a ruthless hand,
Laid waste a great portion of that fair sunny land.
Over ten tribes of Israel, it was now prophesied
Jeroboam as king, should reign and preside.
Then fired with ambition, Jeroboam began
A revolt against Solomon, privately, to plan.

But the king, his treasonable act to prevent,
Officers to arrest him, immediately sent;
Jeroboam forewarned into Egypt then fled,
But in a short time returned, hearing Solomon was dead.
The ten tribes of Israel now determined that he,
Instead of Rehoboam, their ruler should be.
To build a palace at Shechem they also decide,
That their king, Jeroboam, might in it reside.

So Solomon's son, to Jerusalem went,
To rule the two tribes he at last was content.
Although his first impulse, had been to rebel,
Until Shemaiah, the prophet, did the evil foretell.
In addition to this, he was aware of the fact,
That in his ejectment there was considerable tact,
In exacting him to tell, just how he would reign;
If as Israel's king, he was allowed to remain.

To answer them roughly, Rehoboam was inclined,
Which caused his dethronement as previously designed
But the tribes of Judah and Benjamin still cling
To Solomon's son, as their own rightful king.
So Israel now by two kings was led,
And each one the other it seems constantly dread.
And so when the feast of the tabernacles came around,
A new place of worship by Jeroboam was found.

For if his people were allowed, Rehoboam to meet,
He feared it might bring to himself a defeat.

And so then unto them, he does artfully say
Jerusalem from here is too far away.
Two golden calves, with a temple for each,
I'll place where all can easily reach.

This pleasing the people, he does then undertake
A high priest of himself to sacrilegiously make;
But when he commenced the sacrifices to offer,
A prophet this warning did unto them proffer.
A righteous man named Josiah will one day be sent
To punish this evil; for 'tis thus God's intent.
And to prove it to you, God will soon send a token,
For the altar in pieces shall be immediately broken.

Jeroboam in defiance, then stretched out his hand,
Save the altar at once was now his command.
But his arm was paralyzed, and could nothing hold,
While the altar was broken, as Jadon foretold.
Jeroboam now begged the prophet would implore
For God his paralyzed arm to restore.
'Twas done; and then the prophet was invited,
To the home of the king, that he might be requited
For the service he'd done: but the prophet said nay:
God forbade me to tarry, or to return the same way.

And so he departed, but a friend of Jeroboam
Followed, and begged him return to his home:
For, he said, we both being prophets, 'tis right
That you should now stay with me over night.
And so he returned, but learned, when too late,
That a bitter punishment did him await:

For the next morning he was met by a lion, and
    killed;
And thus God's promise unto him was fulfilled.

The false prophet, to the king did this idea convey,
Jadon was an impostor, as his death did portray;
Jeroboam this statement was pleased to believe,
And so from Jadon's warning no good did receive;
But his false hearted friend very well knew,
That what Jadon had said was every word true.

Rehoboam for some time, with such wisdom reigned,
That not only the respect of his own people gained;
But the Levites and others, with Jeroboam disgusted,
Their fortunes with Rehoboam, willingly intrusted.
Whose power increased daily, now by their accessions;
Also he thereby greatly enlarged his possessions.
Thirty concubines, and eighteen wives he possessed,
But Absalom's daughter, of all he loved best.
His preference for her was in this way indicated
Abijah, her son, as his successor he designated.

But now alas Rehoboam forsakes the law of the
    Lord,
And accordingly meets with his proper reward.
A certain king of Egypt, Shishak by name,
To destroy Jerusalem with a great army came:
But Shemaiah, the prophet, to Rehoboam went,
And by predicting results, caused him thus to repent.

Then because of this thing, God would not consent
That Rehoboam's kingdom from him should be rent;

But the Holy Temple, and the kings palace the same,
Their gold and their treasures Egypt's plunder became.
Twelve years after this, Rehoboam sickened and died,
And by his son Abijah his place was supplied;
While he the royal sepulcher was buried within,
As David and Solomon before him had been.

And, although Jeroboam still continues to reign,
Not much longer in peace now will he remain,
For having a sick child, he sends to Shiloh his wife,
To consult with a prophet regarding its life.
This prophet was Ahijah, who unto her said,
Before you return your child will be dead.
For God has determined to punish Jeroboam,
Not only by bringing great sorrow to his home,
But also his enemies shall him utterly defeat,
And the slain of his household the dogs and fowls eat.

As Ahijah prophesied, just so was it done,
Even to the death of King Jeroboam's son;
But the prophet's prediction, so quickly verified,
From Jeroboam's evil ways did not turn him aside,
For to destroy the king of Judah is now his intent,
And so with a large army into his territory went.

But Abijah was brave, notwithstanding his youth,
And in a speech to the people, told them the truth.
With idolatry and sacrilege he Jeroboam charged;
On the division of the tribes he also enlarged.

But while he was talking, by Jeroboam was found
An opportunity his camp to secretly surround.

Now Abijah so implicitly on God did rely,
That he feared not this army to boldly defy,
And although it was twice the size of his own,
A more perfect defeat there never was known.
In Jeroboam's army five hundred thousand were slain,
While Judah from them many cities did gain.

But Abijah lived not his majority to attain,
And only three years was he permitted to reign;
Then he died leaving wives and children behind;
Asa, his son, was his successor we find.
Jeroboam's death, two years after, few mourn;
Of his greatness and power so completely he's shorn.
His successor was Nadab, by his wickedness known,
He died in two years after assuming the throne.
Being killed by Ahijah's son, Baasha by name;
Who over the ten tribes a king then became.

His first act, the words of the prophet fulfilled,
For the entire household of Jeroboam he killed.
And then to vindicate his vainglorious power,
He left them for the dogs and the fowls to devour.
Now how different over Judah was 'Asa's good reign,
As in peace, for ten years, by his wisdom, they remain.
But danger being imminent on nearly every side,
He organized a large army against it to provide.
Soon the king of Ethiopia, with an army immense,
Forces them to fight, which they do in self-defense.

Asa the true God had ever followed and obeyed,
So unto him now he most fervently prayed.
In his prayer with reverence, he expressed the belief
That God, all powerful, would give them relief.
His prayer was answered, the Ethiopians defeated,
And with a great loss they precipitately retreated.

Asa was now permitted to enjoy a long peace;
In his kingdom he forced all idolatry to cease.
Even his own mother he would not allow to be queen,
Because an idol she made by him had been seen.
But while in the thirty-sixth year of his reign,
Baasha, who as ruler over the ten tribes did remain.
With an army in array, threatened Judah to invade,
Whereupon Asa solicited the king of Syria for aid.
Ben-hadad, who although to Baasha a friend,
For a promised reward his armies did send.
Which in a short time, Baasha's army overthrow,
And cause them from Jerusalem quite willingly to go.
But Baasha, in his iniquity, very soon after died,
And by his son Elah, his place was supplied,
Who reigned two years, then was by Zimri assassinated;
For to seize the king's throne had this man anticipated.
Not long unmolested, however, did he reign;
But during the time Baasha's household was slain.

Omri for a king, the army better did please;
So they went to the palace Zimri to seize;
But of their hostile intention he having learned,
Set fire to the palace and in it was burned.

Now followed Omri, who, both wicked and vain,
Reigned a few years, and then, being slain,
Was succeeded by Ahab, a son of his own,
Whose iniquitous deeds will hereafter be shown.

Forty-one years in Jerusalem Asa did reign,
And adjured his people from all evil to abstain;
His own heart he kept perfect in the Lord's sight,
And now, at his death all of Judah unite
In making his burial most solemn and grand,
While, for a king, Jehosaphat supplies the demand.

Like Asa, his father, he walked in God's ways,
And reigned in prosperity all of his days.
But Ahab, who over the other tribes reigned,
In sacrilegious practices the true God disdained;
He married an idolatress, Jezebel by name,
In all of her wickedness an accomplice became.

Among other things which they ordered to be done;
Was to slay the true prophets of God every one.
But Obadiah managed one hundred prophets to save,
By supplying them with food, while they hid in a cave.
To justly punish Ahab was now God's intent,
And to warn him, the prophet Elijah he sent.
Who told him a drought for a period would prevail,
Which would cause vegetation of all kinds to fail.

Now Ahab, being angry, God warned Elijah to hide
By the brook of Cherith, and there awhile to abide.
From the brook he drank, by the ravens was fed;
For so it should be, God had unto him said.

When the brook became dry because of no rain,
God then said arise, here no longer remain.
But go to Zarephath, a widow woman there,
Her sustenance with thee I've commanded to share.

In obedience he went, and met the poor woman thereby,
Who, destitute of food, was expecting to die;
But Elijah assured her 'twas by God's command
He now came to solicit food from her hand.
And so then a cake, to prepare she made haste,
And found in her provisions not a particle of waste.

And so God continued this family to sustain
As long as the famine in the land did remain.
Elijah some time with this woman had stayed,
When dead in the house her only son laid.
To upbraid the prophet was now her first thought,
Saying on me this sorrow you've brought.

So Elijah requested the child he might take,
While praying to God for this poor woman's sake,
To restore the son, to its mother alive;
And God heard his prayer, for the child did revive.
The mother, in gratitude, to Elijah then said,
Man of God thou art, and by the Lord led.

Three years of famine, then God told Elijah to go
To Ahab, in Samaria, and there his power show;
He was met by Obadiah while on his way there,
And so told him of his coming, Ahab to prepare.
Obadiah, realizing the danger, first tried
From his intentions to turn the prophet aside,

But finally consented, for in Ahab's household
Being governor, by him the news should be told.

Then Elijah, when meeting Ahab, did say,
The power of my God I will show you to-day.
At Mount Carmel, two altars now let us make,
And two bullocks, likewise, there we will take;
On the altar of Baal one bullock you'll lay,
To burn it with fire then to your god pray.
God's altar by me alone must be made,
And on it the other bullock then laid.

When they met, four hundred and fifty prophets of Baal
All prayed for fire without any avail.
Twelve barrels of water then Elijah had turned
Over the altar he'd made, and expected now burned;
After which he prayed that God in this test,
Himself to the people would plainly manifest,
And they from idolatry would disgustingly turn,
To serve the true God, also of his ways learn.

While praying a fire from Heaven came out,
And burned the altar with the water all about;
The Lord is God the people then cried,
And to kill the false prophets they quickly decide.
So they were taken to a brook and immediately slain;
After which there came an abundance of rain.
Which Elijah foretold, and then as we read,
With God for this blessing did earnestly plead.

Now Jezebel's heart with anger was filled,
And she ordered that Elijah forthwith should be killed.
But he being forewarned to the wilderness fled;
And then, becoming disheartened wished himself dead.
Worried and exhausted he at length fell asleep,
But an angel over him its vigils did keep.
For when he awoke there was food by his side
With a cruse of water which the Lord did provide.

The food being eaten, strength unto him gave,
So he walked on to Horeb, to abide in a cave.
While resting one day, he heard a voice say,
What doest thou here, and although hidden away,
He promptly answered; then the voice did command:
Go forth to the mountain and before the Lord stand.

So doing as he was bidden, then again the voice spake,
Preceded by signs he could not mistake.
The message was this, go return on thy way;
Anoint Hazael king, for the Syrians to obey.
Then Jehu, that Israel by him may be led,
And Elisha, as prophet, anoint in thy stead.
The impious multitude by them shall be slain;
Seven thousand true worshipers will only remain.

Elijah now departed, and thus Elisha soon found,
In a field with oxen he was plowing the ground,
So he cast upon him his mantle to show,
That, as a prophet of God, he was with him to go.

Now Ahab and Jezebel a crime perpetrate,
Unto Naboth, their neighbor, doth it relate.
His vineyard, Ahab much desiring to own,
Went unto Naboth and his wishes made known.
But Naboth refused with his vineyard to part,
So Ahab returned with a sorrowful heart.

Jezebel then bade him be no longer depressed,
For by him the vineyard should be surely possessed.
So letters she sent, in Ahab's own name,
To the judges in Jezreel, and men of great fame.
Commanding them to fast, and then Naboth to bring,
Charging him of blasphemy, against God, and the king.
Also two sons of Belial for witnesses procure,
That the proof of his crime you now may make sure.
After which, Naboth quite dead shall be stoned,
His vineyard, as a forfeit, then by the king owned.

The wicked deed done, then Elijah prophesied,
In the place where Naboth so unjustly had died
Ahab's blood shall be licked by the dogs of the street,
The body of Jezebel they also shall eat.
Desolation, farthermore, shall be brought to this home,
Ahab's house shall surely be as the house of Jeroboam.

On hearing this prediction Ahab was sore grieved,
And he begged of Elijah it might be reprieved.

So God, through the prophet, was then led to say:
Ahab's house I will spare until his son's day.
Benhadad at this time in Syria doth reign,
And conceives a plan, Israel's kingdom to gain.
With his army the city of Samaria he invested,
And then, through ambassadors, of Ahab requested
He should surrender his wealth, his children and wives;
Thus the city would be spared and likewise their lives.

Ahab abjectly consenting unto his proposal,
Then Benhadad demanded the entire city's disposal.
To consult with his people, is now Ahab's determination,
Which causes to be changed the whole negotiation,
For to resist with one accord, they quickly decide,
And Ahab by their decision thought best to abide.

But had not a prophet encouragement given,
Ahab to despair would ere long have been driven;
By following his advice the Syrians were defeated,
But in a few months their attack was repeated.
With no better success did the Syrians now meet,
For, after a great loss, they were obliged to retreat.

Benhadad for some time now kept himself secreted,
And then of king Ahab for mercy he entreated,
Who promised to spare his life, and then, farthermore,
His cities and throne he would immediately restore.
Then the prophet Micaiah, to Ahab thus spake,
Thy life for Benhadad's the Lord will soon take.

Three years over Judah, Jehosaphat has now reigned,
And although in perfect peace, an army, well trained,
Is ready for the king's service at his first call—
For Jehosaphat is loved and respected by all.
He not only served God, but he also did cause
The rulers of the country to teach Moses' laws.
Indeed, was Jehosaphat a sovereign most kind,
And with all Israel to make peace was also inclined.
So his son, and Ahab's daughter, in wedlock are plighted.
In this way the twelve tribes now seem more united.

Sometime after this, with friendly intent,
Jehosaphat on a visit to Samaria went.
King Ahab great feasts then for him did make;
And told him, also, what he thought to undertake.
For a war with Syria he does now contemplate,
And persuaded Jehosaphat with him to co-operate.
But before they started 'twas Jehosaphat's desire
Of one of God's prophets for instructions to inquire.

Ahab's own prophets had advised him to go,
For that it will please him they very well know.
But Jehosaphat to proceed any farther did refuse,
Until Micaiah, the true prophet, gave them his views.
So Ahab was obliged for this prophet to send,
But he was fearful Micaiah would them evil portend:
For his prediction at the time he pardoned Ben-hadad,
Being fresh in his mind, still made him feel sad.

Micaiah was disposed the truth to withhold,
But upon being pressed, did then a vision unfold,
Which unto king Ahab, quite plainly indicated
To be overcome and slain he most surely was fated.
But one of his own prophets still doth maintain
That he certainly would easily the victory gain.
And so he went forth, yet not without fear,
For as a king in the army he dare not appear.

Thus Israel's king the Syrians thought
Jehosaphat to be, and for his life sought,
But when unto them, with a loud voice, he cried,
They saw their mistake, and turned from him aside.
But Ahab, disguised, and with an armor protected,
Was shot at a venture, at the time undetected.
Thus ended his life, at the close of the day,
Then the army dispersed, and so ended the fray.

When the chariot was washed, in which Ahab died,
Dogs licked up his blood, as had been prophesied.
Then Jehosaphat is rebuked by the prophet Jehu,
Regarding the battle, in his first interview.
Who said, that although he had committed a sin
By aiding a man, who so wicked had been,
That God had him spared, because his previous life
Had been righteous and good, devoid of all strife.

Jehosaphat convinced that these words were all true,
His covenant with God made haste to renew;
He also exhorted his people to obey
And honor the true God, in every possible way.
But the Moabites and Ammonites on hostility bent,
Forty miles from Jerusalem, now pitch their tent.

Then Jehosphat, unto God, did most earnestly pray,
That the destruction of Jerusalem he would mercifully stay.
The people in like manner added their entreaties also,
When God, through a prophet, his loving kindness did show.

He ordered Jehosaphat to set his army in array,
At a place from Jerusalem, only a short distance away.
Then to be not dismayed, nor fear for his fate,
But for the salvation of the Lord to patiently wait.
So Jehosaphat went forth then, in the Lord's name,
And of his saving power a recipient became,
For the enemy, becoming with each other enraged,
Were then in a terrible conflict engaged;
Nor did they desist until they were every one killed,
And the valley with dead men completely was filled.

Jehosophat's whole army for the spoils searched three days,
Then to Jerusalem returned, giving God all the praise.
King Ahaziah was Ahab's successor and son,
The friendship of Jehosophat he desired and won.
Together they built of ships a large fleet,
But with them no success were they permitted to meet,

Peaceful, however, was the remainder of Jehosaphat's life,
For after this time he was free from all strife.
When sixty years old he died, and was laid
In the royal tomb, at Jerusalem made.
Then his son Jehoram reigned in his stead,
Who unto Athalia, the daughter of Ahab, was wed.

SECOND KINGS.

Now the kingdom of Judah we must leave for a spell,
And of Ahaziah's reign over the other tribes tell.
Who inherited the iniquities of Jezebel, also
The weakness of Ahab, his father, did show.
For his sins and idolatry speedy punishment was sent,
First the Moabites came, with hostile intent;
But Ahaziah, in conflicts, no victories did gain,
And he died in two years after beginning his reign.

While descending some stairs, through a lattice he fell,
And then sent to Baalzebub his fate to fortell.
But God told Elijah his messenger to meet,
And say because Jehovah you did not entreat;
The king on his bed, in sickness, shall lie
Until the time God appoints, and then he shall die.

When told to the king, he was by anger possessed,
Therefore fifty men sent, Elijah to arrest;
But the prophet a miracle performed, there and then,
For a fire came from Heaven destroying these men.

So the king three times doth his order repeat,
But the last time his messengers, being more discreet,
That Elijah snould meet them did kindly request,
Which he willingly did, and to their proposal acquiesced
To go to the king. This he did without fear;
First being assured that God was unto him near.

Then repeated to Ahaziah what he first prophesied,
Which was fulfilled at once, for he immediately died
Leaving no issue; as king then became
His brother, who was called Jehoram by name.
We read Elisha with Elijah had usually stayed,
Since a prophet, through him, he had been made;
But Elijah now desired to be entirely alone,
For God had unto him his translation made known.

Accordingly, to a number of different places he went,
But to remain behind, Elisha would not consent.
For what was ordained, he was permitted to foreknow,
And so were the prophets living in Bethel and Jericho,
For with Elisha, we find, they had a private interview,
When both of these places he and Elijah passed through.

On reaching the Jordan, they both crossed on dry land,
For the waters were parted by Elijah's own hand.

And now he conversed with Elisha, quite free,
Asking what shall I do, before I'm taken from thee?
Answered Elisha, on me, I would have you bestow
A double portion of your spirit, ere from me you go.
Said he 'tis a hard thing, but so it shall be,
If plainly my departure you're permitted to see.

While yet they were talking from Heaven there came
A chariot of fire and horses of flame,
Followed by a whirlwind, which did Elijah convey
Into Heaven, there with God and the angels to stay.
And so Elisha perceiving it all very plain,
Only desired a short time there now to remain.

So taking the mantle Elijah had dropped,
Beside the river Jordan with it he stopped,
And the waters he smote with the mantle the same
As Elijah had done, when together they came,
The waters divided, which was an infallible test
That the spirit of Elijah on Elisha did rest

When the prophets of Elijah's translation all learn,
Thinking it quite possible for him to return,
They sent fifty men to search mountain and plain,
But as Elisha well knew their search was in vain.
Now the people of Jericho think the water impure,
Whereupon Elisha, his divine power to make sure,
Casts into the spring some salt from a cruse,
Which renders the water desirable for use.
Now not long after this did he remain in Jericho,
But to the city of Bethel decided to go;

On his way some children came out and said,
In a mocking manner, go up, thou bald head.
Then two she bears from a neighboring wood,
Tare these children, for mocking a prophet so good.

But Elisha purposed not in Bethel long remaining,
So went to Samaria, where Jehoram was reigning;
Whose brother, in dying, left the Moabites unsubdued,
And now the revolt was by their forces renewed.
Jehoram dare not, alone, attempt them to resist;
So he begged of Jehosaphat him to assist,
Who as king over Judah, still doth remain—
For twenty-five years did he in Jerusalem reign.

And now at this time, so it plainly appears,
He had only been reigning about eighteen years.
And although his own kingdom was peacefully inclined,
To help others out of trouble, it seems, was destined.
And so with Jehoram he consented to go,
Who solicited the aid of the king of Edom also.
While marching, they searched for water in vain,
Which caused them, of thirst, to bitterly complain.

To consult with a prophet, Jehosaphat now desired,
When, Elisha appearing, of him he inquired.
Who said, were it not for Jehosaphat's sake,
No entreaties to God for this people I'd make.
But the spirit of the Lord came upon him to say,
Dig trenches all over this place right away.

And into them soon plenty of water will run,
Also a great victory by you shall be won.

The Moabites, seeing the water, for blood it mistook,
And for a terrible slaughter, then rushed out to look.
When, perceiving their mistake, they attempt to retreat,
But their rashness proved fatal, and ruin complete.
Great numbers were slain, their cities were burned,
The king's son offered up, then the Israelites returned,
Each to his own land, Jehoram well pleased,
For the Moabites subdued, his mind was now eased.

The prophet Elisha, now began to manifest,
That of a miraculous power he was surely possessed.
As a miracle he performed, not far from this time,
For a poor widow in distress, although not for a crime;
Her husband, leaving a debt, which she, unable to pay,
The creditor came to take her two sons away:
Indeed, so great, was this poor widow's distress,
That a small pot of oil did she only possess.

Go borrow empty vessels, said Elisha, all you can,
And when you return I'll tell you my plan.
A little of your oil into each vessel turn,
In a very short time the result you will learn.
Every vessel being filled will your debt satisfy;
Also for your support, leave some to lay by.

And now to Elisha, a rich woman being kind,
To repay it, an opportunity he does very soon find.

This childless woman, now mourned for a son;
Elisha assured her, God soon would send one.
So God gave her the son as Elisha prophesied,
But, when nearly grown, it sickened and died.

When this Shunammite mother beheld her child dead,
She took it and laid it on Elisha's own bed;
As a room in her house for him she had kept,
Ever since the first time he came there and slept.
And then she rode away the prophet to procure,
For with God he had power she felt very sure.

Elisha's first thought was his servant to send,
But for the prophet himself, did the woman contend.
So he went to the child and over it prayed,
Then breathed in its mouth while on it he laid;
The child growing warm, unto life did return,
While its mother rejoiced the good news to learn.
Bowed down to Elisha, and at his feet fell,
For the miracle was performed, for his sake she knew well.

The good prophet at Gilgal was now to manifest
The God given power of which he was possessed.
Some poisonous food, was there prepared by mistake;
Which he with some meal, quite harmless did make.
After this we read, one hundred people he fed
With a few ears of corn and twenty loaves of bread.
Elisha next did a most wonderful thing,
A leper to be healed, came to Israel's king.
'Twas Naaman, captain in the army of Benhadad,
Whose wife for a servant a little Hebrew girl had.

Who said, if her master to Elisha would go,
He would heal him of the leprosy, she did very well
  know.

So Benhadad to Jehoram, a letter doth send,
Which, not understanding, did him greatly offend.
Then to the king said Elisha, send this leper to me,
That there's a prophet in Israel, I desire him to see.
And so Naaman came, but quite wroth went away,
For Elisha did not even a hand on him lay;
But ordered, through a messenger, himself being un-
  seen,
Go wash in the Jordan, seven times, and be clean.

Had he told him some difficult or great thing to do,
Or even the rivers of Damascus to go *to*—
But this simple thing did him greatly displease,
And yet to return with this terrible disease,
He was loth; and then his attendant thought best,
The efficacy of the prophet's prescription to test;
Which he did, and then joyfully unto Elisha doth go,
For being healed, he desired his gratitude to show.
He also acknowledged no other God could there be,
But the one over Israel, he plainly could see.

For the services of Elisha, he was anxious to pay,
But the prophet emphatically answered him nay.
Then Naaman, desiring an altar to make,
Begged a small portion of the sacred earth he might
  take.
He had heretofore worshiped idols, he said,
But now he should worship the true God instead.

And so he departed, but was o'ertaken very soon
By the servant of Elisha, who begged a small boon.

In his masters name the petition was made;
And the money, he said, some poor prophets to aid.
The request being granted, Gehazi returned,
But his master the fraud had prophetically discerned,
And told him, for a punishment, the leprosy should cleave
Unto him, as before, it Naaman did leave.
And so out of his presence Gehazi did go
Condemned, and a leper, white as the snow.

Elisha a school for the prophets now taught,
To remove to the Jordan, him they besought.
And while building a house, wherein to dwell,
Into the river an ax accidentally fell.
Then Elisha cast a stick, where some saw it drop,
When immediately it swam and came to the top.

And now Benhadad against Jehoram, war doth declare,
But Jehoram, being warned by Elisha, to beware,
Such precautions for safety were accordingly made,
That a conflict with Syria he was enabled to evade.
The cause of his failure, Benhadad having learned,
To destroy Elisha all his efforts were turned.

So he beseiged the city, where the prophet did live,
No chance for escape he intended to give.
Elisha's trust was in God, but, seeing his servant's dismay,
For some visible sign he does earnestly pray.

The young man then beheld, what quieted his fear,
For chariots of fire with horses, were near.

Then in answer to prayer, the enemy were made blind,
And their way to Elisha were unable to find.
So he to Samaria, then led them astray,
Where Jehoram would have slain them, but Elisha said nay.
To this city by me, they have been unwittingly led,
And now I desire that they all shall be fed.
Being no longer blind, they can then easily return;
How this kindness was repaid we shall very soon learn.

To take the city of Samaria, was Benhadad impressed;
Accordingly with a large army, he did it invest,
And so long fresh supplies he managed to exclude,
That a very great famine soon thereby ensued.
King Jehoram the situation did not fully realize,
Until hearing one day a poor woman's cries,
Who for herself and a neighbor had cooked her own son,
The neighbor, the next day, the same should have done;
For so was the compact between the said two,
But the neighbor refused now her part to do.

Jehoram, hearing this, rent his clothes in deep grief,
Also blamed Elisha, for not coming to his relief.
So he ordered an executioner to cut off his head.
But Elisha, forewarned, to his attendants thus said,

Hold the man, for the king will surely repent;
Which he did, and to stay it, himself hastily went.
Then Elisha with compassion, on the morrow foretold,
A measure of flour for a shekel shall be sold.
The king's lord scoffing, did light of this make,
Thou shalt see, said Elisha, but shalt not partake.

Four lepers were sitting without Samaria's gate,
And starving, were therefore indifferent to fate.
So they determined to the Syrian camp they would go;
For to die they were doomed unless spared by the foe.
To their surprise in the camp they found not a man;
Then to capture the spoils they immediately began.
God had frightened these Syrians, with a noise very great,
To save themselves, therefore, they did only await.

'Twas night, and the lepers apprehended no surprise,
But decided at length, perhaps 'twould be wise
To go to the king, and the joyful news spread;
But Jehoram at first fearing danger ahead,
Five horsemen sent, to see if the enemy were near,
What they saw on the road dispelled every fear.
For their garments were scattered along the wayside,
As far as the horsemen were directed to ride.

So the Israelites went to the camp and there found
Flour and other provisions did plentifully abound:
And thus, as Elisha had truthfully foretold,
A measure of flour was for one shekel sold.
Also the king's lord met a sorrowful fate,
Being trode on and killed while guard at the gate.

Regarding Elisha's prophecy we shall now write,
Which he made to the woman called Shunammite.
'Twas foretelling a seven year's famine, and also
To some other land he advised her to go.
As Elisha had restored unto this woman her son,
What he advised her to do was immediately done.

After remaining seven years she returned, but her lands
Had wrongfully passed into other people's hands;
So the woman for her rights appealed to the king,
And to prove her identity did Elisha's servant bring.
The trespassers were removed, and then, farthermore,
All her land and its profits, the king did restore.

Now Benhadad being ill, sent an officer of his court
To Elisha, with a present, his case to report.
Thus Hazael, with forty loaded camels set out
The issue of the king's illness, to learn all about.
But Elisha, somewhat evasively, made this reply:
He mayest recover, but I'm certain he'll die.

And then weeping said, to Hazael, I now see
All the evil that Israel shall suffer from thee;
For God has revealed this thing unto me,
That king over Syria very soon you will be.
When Hazael returned to the king he did say—
You will surely recover, but on the next day
He suffocated Benhadad, with a wet cloth on his face,
Then as king over Syria himself took his place.

Five years Jehoram over Israel had reigned,
When Jehosaphat to die by God was ordained.
Then his son, Jehoram reigned in his stead,
And so the two kingdoms were contemporaneously led
By kings named Jehoram, one Jehosaphat's son;
While Ahab of Samaria was father to the other one.

The son of Jehosaphat over Judah did reign,
But, unlike his father, he was wickedly profane;
And unto Athalia, the daughter of Ahab being wed,
Into all of her wickedness he was easily led:
But his sins deprived him of prosperity and peace;
Eight years he reigned, and then came his decease.

The prophet Elijah, a short time before he died,
Of his downfall and ruin truly prophesied.
He was buried in Jerusalem, not in the royal tomb,
Then his son Ahaziah reigned in his room.
Who reigning one year, with Jehoram then went
Against Hazael, to Syria, with hostile intent.

Jehoram being wounded in the first battle fought,
To Jezreel, to be treated, was accordingly brought.
So Ahaziah, king of Judah, went to visit him there,
While to dispossess them both does Elisha prepare.
For the house of Ahab to destruction was fated,
Since the vineyard of Naboth was by him confiscated.

Although Ahab by entreaty, a short reprieve won,
God said it most surely would come to his son:
And since king Ahaziah, was following the lead—
Of Athalia, his mother, also Jehoram, we read,

Neither one should be rulers, Elisha well knew;
So as king over Israel was anointed Jehu.

For a ruler, by the people, he was joyfully received;
Then to destroy the wicked kings, a plan he conceived.
They now being in Jezreel, and Jezebel also,
With a large army, king Jehu, there started to go.
By Ahaziah and Jehoram being met on the way,
With a bow and an arrow he did them both slay.

Jezebel of her danger, having before been apprised,
Herself as a servant, then cunningly disguised;
But her curiosity overcame her discretion, and so
At an upper window she sat and gazed down below.
And then perceiving Jehu, to rebuke him she thought,
But destruction on herself immediately brought.

For 'twas Jezebel's voice, he did very well know,
And ordered from the window, some one her to throw;
Three eunuchs were standing close at her hand,
Who immediately obeyed king Jehu's command.
Her body was mangled, her flesh the dogs ate;
As Elijah prophesied, then so was her fate.

But seventy sons of Ahab there still did remain,
All of which Jehu ordered very soon to be slain.
After this every one of his household was killed,
Thus the prophecy now was completely fulfilled.
Forty-two brethren of Ahaziahs were next executed;
It would seem Jehu's orders, were now undisputed.

And now soon with Jehonadab chancing to meet,
He invites him to take in his chariot a seat,
To witness, in Samaria, his zeal for the Lord,
First having learned their minds well accord.
When reaching the city, all the worshipers of Baal,
He ordered to meet him, in their temple without fail.
Then he instructed Jehonadab, that each might be known,
To clothe them in vestments, all of which were their own.

These worshipers of idols, were by Jehu deceived;
That he sympathized with them, they fully believed.
And so they all came, but none went away;
For Jehu's executioners did every one slay.
The temple was destroyed, the images burned,
Thus Israel from idolatry was unto God turned.

But king Jehu after this, fell into evil ways,
And in turmoil and strife spent the rest of his days.
By Hazael, in Israel, great havoc was made;
And all of western Palestine under tribute he laid.
As king twenty-eight years, Jehu continued to reign,
Then dying, with Samaria's rulers was lain.

His son, Jehoahaz, reigned in his stead,
And throughout his dominion a wicked life led.
In every battle, by Hazael, he was some way defeated;
And quite like a vassal by him was treated.

Nevertheless, seventeen years he was permitted to reign,
And then with his fathers, in Samaria was lain.
We learn that after him, his son, Joash by name,
Immediately as ruler over Israel became.

But again unto Judah, we now will return,
And who followed Ahaziah, first let us learn.
A fine infant son he left living, it appears,
Who was secreted by his aunt the whole of six years;
For Athalia, her mother, desiring to reign,
Otherwise would have caused the child to be slain.
The young king was anointed, when seven years of age,
Which disenthroned Athalia, and did her enrage.
But the people determined their king to sustain,
So Jehoida, the priest, ordered Athalia to be slain.

Now the king over Judah was Joash by name,
Over Israel, we have learned, 'twas also the same.
But a king thirty-six years, was Ahaziah's young son,
Before Joash to reign over Israel had begun.
While Joash over Judah, by the high priest was led,
The king over Israel followed idolaters instead.
And yet with regret, we must truthfully say,
After Jehoida's death, Joash of Judah went astray.

Now the king of Israel set about to repair
The devastations Benhadad and Hazael wrought there.
The aged prophet Elisha he visits to consult;
And by slighting his directions, this was the result.

When asking if victorious, with the Syrians he should
  be,
He was directed to shoot one arrow and see.

The rest in his quiver to throw on the ground,
But he threw only three as Elisha soon found.
So the Syrians three times, he was only to defeat—
His disobedience prevented their ruin complete.
But Elisha after this never more prophesied,
For being ill at the time he very soon died.

Now the Moabites, by invasion, great desolation
  brought.
'Twas during this time a singular miracle was
  wrought.
A dead comrade, some Moabites intended burying
  one day,
Being frightened, in a sepulcher they hid it away;
'Twas Elisha's and the dead man stood on his feet
When his flesh with the bones of Elisha did meet.

Joash with the Syrians many battles doth fight,
In three great conflicts, he beat them outright;
After which, to great straits he was many times
  driven,
For the victory to the Syrians was continuously
  given.
But before dying, by him all the cities were pos-
  sessed
That Hazael of Syria from his father did wrest.

He also attacked Jerusalem, causing to fall,
Six hundred feet, of that city's high wall;

Then spoiled the temple, of its silver and gold,
But of his history after this, not much are we told,
Except he was buried in Samaria his home,
And was succeeded by his son, a second Jeroboam.

Now Joash over Judah, some years had been dead,
And his son Amaziah, had reigned in his stead—
The greater part of the time, Jehoahaz's son,
By the death of his father, the scepter had won.
But before Amaziah, succeeded to the throne,
Joash, his father, his reverence had shown:
By ordering the priests and Levites to repair
The Temple, which the sons of Athalia made bare.
Thus a proclamation was made throughout the land,
For contributions from the people to supply the demand.
Jehoida, the high priest, assisted the temple to repair,
And during his life the offerings were made there;
But after his death, Joash, strangely to say,
The Lord's house did forsake, and from him turned away.
So God sent his prophets this people to warn,
But their prophecies were unheeded and treated with scorn.
Then Jehoida's son came in the spirit of the Lord,
But they stoned him to death as a reward,
Which, if not executed by Joash's own hand,
It was certainly subject to his command.

And now as a judgment from God, Judah's sins to requite,
Came the Syrian army, this kingdom to smite;

Also Joash, on his bed with sickness and pain,
For his infamous deeds by his servants is slain.
He was buried in Jerusalem in his forty-seventh year,
So reigned forty years it doth plainly appear.

Amaziah, like his father his reign began well,
And then, like him, at last, into sinful ways fell.
In battle he was permitted great victories to win;
But his prosperity seemed to prompt him to sin,
For which he was punished, as had been prophesied,
Being slain by conspiracy, and thus ignominiously died:
Then his son Azariah, only sixteen years old,
As king over Judah the scepter did hold.

Now Jeroboam over Israel sixteen years had been reigning,
So of his forty-one years there were twenty-five remaining.
Fifty-two years in Jerusalem Azariah was king,
And his wisdom to Judah, doth prosperity bring.
But notwithstanding this, during the latter part of his reign,
The house of the Lord he did wilfully profane;
As a leper he was smitten, then by God's hand,
And Jotham, his son, judged the people of the land.

Jeroboam, king of Israel during his reign,
Successfully strove his dominions to regain.
For the Syrians over Israel had made many a conquest,
Until the lands east of Jordan were by them possessed.

But these lands were recovered before Jeroboam died,
And he also captured Ammon and Moab beside.

Immediately after him his son Zachariah did reign,
But by Shallam, in six months, was treacherously slain.
Who reigned only a month, and then he was fated,
By Menahem, son of Gadi, to be assassinated.
For ten years over Israel was this wicked man king,
While of him recorded we find no good thing.
What at last caused his death we never have read,
But that his son Pekahiah reigned in his stead.
Two years Pekahiah his father's place filled,
And then in his palace, by Pekah, was killed,
Whose father, a captain, his company brought there,
And of the men in the palace not any did spare.

So now Pekah was king, having Pekahiah deposed,
About the same time, Azariah's reign closed;
And, during his reign, the Assyrians manage to wrest
From Israel, a great share of the land they possessed.
This idolatrous man was allowed the rulership to retain
Twenty years, and then by Hoshea was slain;
Jotham king of Judah, reigned about sixteen years,
And exalted the kingdom, so it appears.
But Ahaz, his son, who reigned in his stead,
By idolatrous practices was all his life led.

A rich district of his dominions, the Syrians occupied,
But he could not recover it, he was well satisfied,
So to secure the friendship of the Assyrian king,
The treasures of the temple, he did unto him bring.
Thus, no reverence for God's house Ahaz doth show,
And for it, by Jehovah, he was justly brought low.

Turmoil and strife all his days was his doom,
At his death Hezekiah reigned in his room.
In the twelfth year of Ahaz, Hoshea assassinated,—
Pekah, king of Israel, as before we have stated,
Then, as Israel's king, all manner of evil he wrought,
In his ninth year the kingdom was to an end brought.

The Assyrians of the people now captives all make,
Then come to their cities, their possessions to take;
So the Israelites were carried from their own land away,
No tribe, except Judah, was permitted to stay.
Over them, Hezekiah six years had been reigning,
So unto him three and twenty years were remaining.

The evils of his father, he strove to make right,
And did that which was pleasing in the Lord's sight.
Some priests he appointed the temple to repair;
After cleansing, the sacrifices then were made there.

Using David's own words, the Levites sang praise,
And the true God was worshiped as in Solomon's days.

Then for all to be present, an invitation was sent,
For to keep the passover, by Hezekiah was meant.
So then came all of Judah this memorial to renew,
While the idols and images into the Kidron they threw.
Then the people were commanded tithes they should bring,
To encourage the priests in every good thing.

Fourteen years peace and plenty reigned in the land,
Then Judah was spoiled, by the Assyrian king's hand;
The walled cities, save Jerusalem, being taken every one,
Then embassadors were sent to see what could be done.
For five hundred thousand dollars, the king did agree,
From the ravages of his army, to leave Jerusalem free.
Never doubting his word, the money was paid,
But the treacherous king their confidence betrayed.

For to demand another tribute, a large army he sent,
Who with threats of destruction, were not then content,
But did God also blaspheme, and with Hezekiah find fault,
At the same time, their false gods sought to exalt.

But Hezekiah taught his people on Jehovah to depend;
And to the prophet Isaiah for counsel did send.
He also earnestly prayed, and when the messengers returned,
For the safety of Jerusalem he was no longer concerned.

As the prophecy assured, God would help right away,
Which he did at the close of that very same day—
Of the Assyrians, one hundred and eighty-five thousand died,
While the remainder all fled, by the plague terrified.
The king was now spared, but not long permitted to reign,
For by his two sons he was soon treacherously slain.

After this, king Hezekiah, on a sick bed confined,
Was warned of his death, that he might be resigned.
The prophet Isaiah was the messenger sent;
But Hezekiah was disposed his fate to lament;
So God, knowing his heart, and hearing his prayer,
Promised his life fifteen years longer to spare.

The king of Babylon, pretending anxiety for his health,
But really to learn all about his great wealth,
Sent embassadors with letters, and a present also,
To Hezekiah, who foolishly his treasures did show:
For his vanity and imprudence then Isaiah came to say,
Your possessions into Babylon shall be carried away.

Hezekiah being grieved, vehemently prayed
That, during his life, the prophecy be stayed.
Then to improve Jerusalem, the rest of his years,
With assiduity he worked, so it recorded appears.
By Manasseh he was succeeded, his twelve year old
 son;
Indeed, as we find he had only this one.
Fifty-five years, in Jerusalem, Manasseh is king,
And his wickedness for a time great evils doth bring.
But his continued afflictions caused him at last to
 repent,
And his remaining years were in pious deeds spent.

After him, his son Ammon two years only did reign,
And then, by his servants, was treacherously slain;
But the conspirators, by the people were immedi-
 ately killed,
And Josiah, at eight years, his father's place filled.
A loving disposition he manifested in youth,
And, believing in God, he sought after the truth.

The temple he repaired, and the false gods destroyed;
In the expulsion of idolatry he was mostly employed.
The holy books of Moses, by the priest being found,
Josiah after reading, sought their truths to expound.
So both king and people, now in the Lord's sight,
Covenanted and agreed to do that which was right.

For the sins of the people, Josiah well knew,
God's punishment justly was unto them due;
But the thought, nevertheless, caused him much
 grief,
So of the prophetess Huldah, he sought for relief,

Who, truthfully to console him, could only this say—
The punishment must come, but not in *your* day.
So Josiah, while living, did every possible thing
To destroy the evil works of Jeroboam when king.

Thirty-one years, in Jerusalem, does this pious man reign,
And then by the Egyptians in battle is slain.
On his death, lamentations Jeremiah did write,
While with him, to mourn, all of Judah unite.
The death of king Josiah was a great loss indeed,
For although his son Jehoabaz did him succeed,
Unlike his father, he was both wicked and vain,
And only three months was permitted to reign.

For the king of Egypt did now Judah subjugate,
And to be taken away was Jehoabaz's fate.
His brother Eliakim then, with a changed name,
Over Judah a king immediately became.
But Jehoiakim, like his brother, was wickedly inclined,
And under a heavy tribute, the Egyptians him bind.

He was also a servant unto Nebuchadnezzar three years,
So not much more than a vassal unto us he appears;
For after rebelling against the Babylonian king,
Then the Lord against *him* other nations did bring.
Thus he reigned eleven years, amid turmoil and strife,
After which, as a captive, he ended his life.

Then Jehoiachin, his son, now eighteen years old,
The scepter three months was only suffered to hold.

Then king Nebuchadnezzar, who successful had been,
And permitted a great many conquests to win,
With a vast army came, and did Jerusalem invest,
Eighteen hundred people captured, the king with
    the rest.

Then his uncle Zedekiah reigned in his stead,
And Judah eleven years was by this wicked king led.
The prophet Jeremiah, and other messengers God
    sent,
To warn this wicked people of their sins to repent;
But the prophets were mocked and abused by them all,
Until the judgments of God upon them must fall.
So Jerusalem was besieged, by the Babylonian king,
And the city was spoiled of every valuable thing.

After robbing the temple, Jerusalem was burned,
Then unto the people, the king's attention is turned;
Zedekiah's eyes were put out, and he into prison cast,
While the sentence of death on his people was passed.
Only the poor of the land did the Syrians spare,
The vine dressing and husbandry was left in their care.

But a very short time did they in Judah remain,
For their ruler, with a multitude of others being slain,
To flee into Egypt, the remnant made haste.
Thus Judah uninhabited seventy years was left waste:
But the Jews in Egypt, did not very long stay,
For by Nebuchadnezzar they were taken away,
And remained in Babylon, so it appears,
Until before Christ, five hundred and thirty-six years.

Ezra.

We shall next write in Ezra, as our readers will find,
That Chronicles and Kings have been together combined.
Now the Jews in bondage seventy years having passed.
God sends unto them a deliverer at last.
'Twas Cyrus, king of Persia, and Darius also,
Who the Babylonian king together overthrow.
Thus the Jews held as captives by Belshazzar then,
Fall into the hands, of these two pious men.

Then Cyrus, by the spirit of the Lord being stirred,
Throughout his whole kingdom sent forth this word:
A temple in Jerusalem, God has charged me to build.
Now who is there among you, with his love being filled,
Who will help in the work, also contributions make,
That the building of the temple we may safely undertake?
The Jews their enthusiasm now unreservedly show,
And nearly all, to Jerusalem, are ready to go.

The rich gifts and vessels, by Nebuchadnezzar carried away,
Nearly equal the collections in Solomon's day.
And these now added to the contributions, it would seem
All things were favorable for the beginning of the scheme.
So nearly fifty thousand Jews for Jerusalem departed,
And as quickly as possible the temple was started.

The priests and the Levites as directors were made,
And they also sang praises, when the foundation was laid.

The adversaries of Judah, of the building having heard,
To assist in the work, to the overseers sent word.
These people were Samaritans, who from Assyria immigrated
At the time Israel's kingdom was utterly exterminated.
And although moral and just, they were idolators nevertheless,
So the Jews being anxious their work God should bless,
Their kind offer rejected, thus the Samaritans conspire,
To hinder their work, and for it counsellors hire.

At the death of king Cyrus, to his successor they send
Letters concerning the Jews, which to them evil portend.
Their representations with Artaxerxes had considerable influence,
So he ordered in the building no further pursuance.
But Darius very soon did Artaxerxes succeed
And that the work should go on by him was decreed.
So the temple was finished without any arrears,
Before Christ, as we learn, about five hundred and fifteen years.

Then as in Solomon's days, the temple was dedicated;
The Jews in the services, all joyfully participated,
And although at this time, they purposed God to obey,
From the laws of Moses they all afterward stray;
So Ezra of Babylon, did king Xerxes beseech,
That he might go to Jerusalem, there Moses' law teach.
The king of Persia, not only willingly granted his request,
But sent money in offerings, unto God to invest;
Also a letter to the Jews, by Ezra he sent—
To protect and sustain them, was its portent.

But when Ezra departed, he went not alone,
For to the Jews left in Babylon, Xerxes made known
That for all who desired, he had provided a way
To go to Jerusalem, with their brethren to stay.
So a large company went, and when there, Ezra found
The Jews had taken wives from the nations all around.

Now both priest and scribe in Babylon he had been,
So he prayed unto God to remedy this sin.
When the people wept sore, and unto him said,
We will now put away the strange wives we have wed;
For to remedy this evil they no other way saw,
Thus in time 'twas accomplished according to law.

NEHEMIAH.

We find that Nehemiah in Persia still stayed;
For as a cup bearer to Xerxes he had been made.

But to assist his brethren was his greatest desire;
Thus for the cause of his sadness the king doth inquire.
So Nehemiah, unto Xerxes, opened his heart,
And begged for Jerusalem he would allow him to start.
Also to assist him, his plan to carry out,
Which was to build a new wall the city all about.

Nehemiah for his brethren, had oft inquiries made,
And for them likewise, had most vehemently prayed.
So when the king granted very willingly his request,
He felt by God's hand that he had been blessed.
After reaching Jerusalem and inspecting the old wall,
He apportioned the work unto the different families all;
But, as when building the Temple, their enemies deride,
And seek in every way their work to put aside.

But their threats on Nehemiah were devoid of effect,
For he trusted that God would this people protect;
Yet an army was stationed the city all around,
Which if danger threatened, were their trumpets to sound.
So the building progressed, with Nehemiah to superintend,
On whom at this time, the Jews seem to depend.

The people, we learn, by taxation were distressed,
Many having mortgaged everything they possessed:

Even then, the tribute, some unable to pay,
Their children as servants, were taken away.
But these persecutions Nehemiah put to an end,
By inducing the rulers their laws to amend.

The enemy now to attack the Jews openly fear,
And accordingly as rebels seek to make them appear.
But in answer to prayer, God did them sustain,
And enabled Nehemiah the king's confidence to retain.
So in some over two years after 'twas begun,
Not only the wall but the gates were all done.

Its completion by a feast, they now celebrated,
Soon after the anniversary of their release was commemorated.
Regarding Moses' law, Ezra read some each day,
And for the blessings of God he also did pray.
While the people all weeping their heads in reverence bow,
For their sins and transgressions they plainly see now.

But Nehemiah entreated them their sorrow to cease,
For the joy of the Lord was unto them peace;
With these comforting words their hearts were made light,
And they set about doing that which was right.
The Levites and priests a solemn confession now make,
And the house of the Lord promise never to forsake.
That they should live in Jerusalem, Nehemiah desired,
After building the number of houses required.

Then he ordered tithes brought by those living outside,
For to maintain public worship ne sought to provide.
To desecrate the Sabbath, some being disposed,
The gates of the city on that day were now closed.
We read Nehemiah in Jerusalem was governor twelve years,
And as a pious reformer at all times appears.

ESTHER.

Ahasuerus, king of Persia three years had been reigning,
When friends in his palace he was royally entertaining;
The riches of his kingdom he did proudly display;
After which, being made with wine very gay,
His messengers he sent in quest of the queen.
That her beauty by all of his guests could be seen.
Queen Vashti was holding a banquet also,
And being modest, refused with the messengers to go.
Which angered the king, who his wise men then saw,
To see what could be done, according to law.
So fearing other wives would their lords disobey,
They advised Ahasuerus to put Vashti away.

Then fair virgins throughout the kingdom were sought,
That before Ahasuerus they at once could be brought:
The one he selected to take the queen's place,
Was Esther, a Jewess, with a beautiful face.
The king of her nationality never thought to inquire,
For to make her his wife was his greatest desire.

Mordecai, being to Esther a relative near,
And she a lone orphan, he had taken her to rear.
The king's palace at Shushan was now situated,
And Mordecai, to move there, at once contemplated.
Soon after his removal he saved the king's life,
By disclosing a conspiracy through Esther, his wife.

The conspirators were killed, and the circumstance noted,
* But Haman, in the place of Mordecai was promoted;
So when the people, in reverence, to Haman bowed low,
Mordecai unto him no reverence did show.
Then Haman being angry, to Ahasuerus went,
For the destruction of Mordecai, was now his intent.

So well he succeeded, that on a certain day,
Every Jew in the kingdom, 'twas the king's order, to slay.
Now this thing to Mordecai, was grievous indeed,
So he desired that Esther would with the king plead;
'Twas contrary to law, but she consented at last,
Requiring three days they together should fast.

The third day, in her royal apparel being dressed,
Esther stood before the king, to make her request;
Her presence with pleasure, did Ahasuerus inspire,
And so of the queen's wishes, he was fain to inquire.
He also encouraged her, to lay all timidity aside;
For whatsoever she desired, it should not be denied.

So she invited the king, in a most cordial way,
Accompanied by Haman, to a feast that same day.

To the banquet they came, and then the king pressed
The queen to make known unto him her request.
She said on the morrow, my petition I'll make,
If with me, at a feast, again you'll partake.
This was pleasing to the king, and made Haman proud,
And yet, there was over his pathway a cloud.

For notwithstanding the Jews were so soon to be slain,
Mordecai still treated him with perfect disdain.
Nor was he quite sure what might be *his* fate,
As Mordecai, each day, sat at the king's gate.
So by the advice of his friends, likewise his wife,
He decided of the king to ask for Mordecai's life.
Then a gallows he ordered, made fifty cubits high,
That on it, Mordecai, should hang till he die.

The records being read to Ahasuerus that night,
Mordecai's kind act, he thought best to requite.
So Haman he consulted as to what should be done,
Some honor to confer upon a loved one.
Haman thought surely, that one must be me;
And so his advice and his honors gave free.
But when the whole truth, by Haman was learned,
His joy into grief very quickly was turned.

But while to his wife the story he was relating,
He was told that Queen Esther's banquet was waiting.
So he hasted away, but he dreamed not his fate,
How soon death on the gallows did him await.

For, when to the king Esther made her petition,
He saw very plain what had been her condition,
And that Haman, who, desiring Mordecai to spite,
Had wickedly planned the Jews all to smite.

So Haman on the gallows he'd prepared for Mordecai,
Was destined to be hanged and ignominiously die.
Then Mordecai was exalted to take Haman's place,
While favor was shown unto those of his race—
Who under subjection to the terrible decree,
Had expected so soon their destruction to see;
Indeed the king left it, for Mordecai to write,
For the Jews, whatsoever was pleasing in his sight.

So he gave them permission on a specified day,
To prepare for an attack, thus their enemies to slay.
So these Hebrew people a great victory now gain,
For seventy-five thousand Amalekites by them were slain.
Also Haman's ten sons, by queen Esther's request,
Were hanged, ere the Jews from their labors did rest.

After which, their deliverance, by a feast they celebrate,
Which by Mordecai's orders they are to forever commemorate.
Mordecai, by Ahasuerus, was shown favor through life,
Not only because he was a relative of his wife;
But his influence was good, and peace he did bring,
To his own people the Jews, and likewise the king.

JOB.

In the land of Uz, there lived a person, Job named,
And although, for his riches, this man was far-famed,
His righteousness exceeded his wealth, we are told,
While he also possessed quite a numerous household.
Seven sons, and three daughters were this father's delight ;
And he taught them religiously to walk in God's sight.

But Satan, desiring Job's righteousness to test,
Insisted he was good, because of the wealth he possessed :
Then that Job shall be persecuted, God does permit;
Feeling sure, that this pious man will patiently submit.
So his riches take wings, his sons and daughters lay dead,
And although mourning for his children, he submissively said:
God hath given and now he hath taken away;
Blessed be God, he did furthermore say.

Now Satan perceiving, he submitted with grace,
Vowed he could make him curse God to his face.
His flesh and his bone he would touch he now said;
And covered him with boils from his feet to his head.
'Twas permitted, yet not at the expense of his life,
But to curse God and die he was advised by his wife.
Said Job, thou talkest as a foolish woman should,
For how can we expect to receive nothing but good.

And now three wise men came with him to mourn,
But Job's heart with anguish, at last, seems to be torn,
For he curses the day of his birth, and also
Thinks to his grave 'twould be pleasant to go.
Then follows a discussion, very interesting indeed,
But which to appreciate, we must every one read

His friends in the law of retribution persist;
And that his afflictions are due to some sin, they insist;
In God's justice and Omnipotence Job did firmly believe:
But that both just and sinful his mercies receive;
And that his punishment and rewards, in some future day,
God would surely mete out in his own proper way.
But, by argument, he becomes somewhat impatient at last,
And speaks of his good deeds done in the past;
Thus, while in the Lord his faith still is unshaken,
To justify himself, he has foolishly undertaken.

And now another friend seeks them all to impress
That some wisdom quite wonderful he does possess;
But God, in a whirlwind, now coming to speak,
Job thus beholds himself as a being quite weak.
His humility and penitence, God seeing with pleasure,
Of earthly blessings he gives him, now, a double measure.

But rebuking his friends, he did unto them say,
Take an offering to Job, then for you he'll pray,

For your acts are displeasing still in my sight,
And what you have spoken is far from being right.
Very willing was Job for his friends all to pray,
As his faith was being strengthened in God every day.
After this, with great wealth he again was possessed,
And with both sons and daughters, likewise, he was blessed.
His age at this period, in no place appears,
But after it, we learn, he lived one hundred and forty years.

PSALMS.

These beautiful songs David mostly did write;
In supplication and praises they all do unite.
We shall not speak of them separately, but as a whole;
They seem a melodious cure for the soul.
For so precious and Christ-like do they appear,
'Tis, no matter how oft' they fall on the ear,
New beauties and truths we perceive in them each time;
Indeed, they are grandly, beautifully sublime.

PROVERBS.—ECCLESIASTES.—SOLOMON'S SONG.

Proverbs, Ecclesiastes and Solomon's song,
In one book all together properly belong,
For surely they were said to be written every one,
By Solomon, whom we know, was unto David a son;
These writings his divine wisdom forcibly exemplify,
And to follow them *all* will be profited thereby.

DANIEL.

The book of Daniel, we find, a partial history doth give
Of the Jews, while as captives in Babylon they live.
Three thousand were taken captive and a great many slain
At the time Jehoiakim over Judah did reign.
'Twas by Nebuchadnezzar, who had the brightest ones brought
To the royal palace, the Chaldean language to be taught.

Then a daily provision of the king's wine and meat,
He desired these pupils for three years to eat.
Now Daniel, and three of his young companions beside,
To eat the king's food were not at all satisfied,
So of the prince of the eunuchs does Daniel entreat
For water to drink, also pulse they might eat.

This man had been unto Daniel a friend,
And yet he was fearful Nebuchadnezzar to offend,
As he supposed these pupils would very thin grow,
And thereby to the king their keeping would show.
But they were finally promised a ten day's test,
At the end of which time were fairer than the rest.

Great knowledge, also, God gave unto these four,
Which the following names respectively bore:
Belteshazzar for Daniel, Shadrach for Hananiah,
Meshach for Mishael, and Abednego for Azariah.
In this manner these names I have written and arranged,
So all will understand how they have been changed.

At the end of three years the learning of these four,
Compared with the others appeared ten times more.
In all visions and dreams had Daniel understanding.
Now the king had a dream, great wisdom demanding,
For the dream had nearly escaped from his mind,
And so to interpret it no one could he find.
Then the king determined this proclamation to make,
The lives of the wise men I will every one take.

When Daniel, having heard of this hasty decree,
If the king would give time, went immediately to see.
For, if so, he promised to interpret his dream,
Although to the Chaldeans it does impossible seem.
But Daniel, going to his companions, this to them doth say,
For the secret, together, we must unto God pray.

It came, in a vision, to Daniel in the night,
The dream, and interpretation, both proved to be right.
With humility Daniel did unto Nebuchadnezzar declare,
'Twas not of himself, but in answer to prayer.
The kingdoms of the world, in the dream were foreshown;
Also the coming of Christ, it did plainly make known.
And that *his* kingdom forever and ever should stand,
While the others were to be broken and consumed by his hand.

With Daniel's divine nature, now the king was impressed;
And that *his* God was supreme, he also confessed.

So of Daniel, he made a ruler very great;
And likewise permitted him to sit in his gate.
Then Daniel requested, he should some honor bestow,
On Shadrach, Meshach and also Abednego.

But Nebuchadnezzar had a golden image made,
And on the people of his realm, this injunction he laid,
Before this image, you shall bow to the ground,
Upon hearing a chorus of musical instruments sound.
In case of disobedience, *this* sentence was passed,
He that faileth shall immediately in a fiery furnace be cast.

To commit this sin, Daniel's companions refuse;
Then the king, in a fury, commanded these Jews,
By his strongest men, to be bound and made fast,
After which, in the furnace of fire to be cast.
This furnace had been heated seven times more
Than ever it was known to have been before.

Indeed 'twas so hot that the king's men were slain,
While over the furnace they were obliged to remain.
But the king was astonished when he afterward found
These Jews in the furnace, unharmed and unbound.
And instead of three men, there now appeared four,
While one, the form of the Son of God bore.

Then he said to the men, come hither to me;
For as servants of God, he now knew them to be.
To worship their God, he did also truly desire,
Who was able to save men even from fire.

So he made a decree his vengeance to wreak
On any, who against the true God should speak.
Then for the wrong he had done, to make some amends,
He immediately promoted Daniel's three friends.

Now in a very short time, another vision had the king,
Which unto his remembrance every word he could bring;
So for the wise men of Babylon he accordingly sent,
But not one of them was competent to give its portent:
Then he sent for Daniel, whom he knew very well,
The import of the dream could readily tell.

Daniel seeing the dream did evil portend,
Hesitated awhile, fearing Nebuchadnezzar to offend.
But being assured by the king he had nothing to fear,
He truthfully revealed what to him was made clear,
The king had transgressed, in some way it appears,
And so was to be exiled from men seven years.

With the beasts of the field, he was destined to live,
The grass that they ate, would him nourishment give.
But his kingdom was to be given back in that day,
When he acknowledged that God over earth held the sway;
Then Daniel unto the king some good council gave,
Which would tend his tranquility to lengthen and save

But twelve months after, in his palace he was walking,
And of his own greatness vain-gloriously talking;
When a voice from Heaven, Daniel's words reiterated,
And that his kingdom had departed, it furthermore stated.
So king Nebuchadnezzar, that very same day,
Was driven from home, seven years an exile to stay.
But he returned with a heart overflowing with praise
Unto God, who prospered him the rest of his days.
Over Babylon he reigned, forty-three years as a king,
And the world under subjection to himself he did bring.

Of Belshazzar's feast, in this book we next read,
Whom it seems, as a king, did his father succeed,
And that the vessels taken from the temple he profaned,
While, at this same feast, one thousand lords he entertained.
During the revelry, a man's fingers were discerned
Writing on the wall, what puzzled the most learned.

Then to send for Daniel, the queen doth advise,
While of his divine wisdom she does them apprise.
And when Daniel came, he first related to the king,
The punishment God on Nebuchadnezzar did bring.
Then he rebuked Belshazzar for his *own* wicked deed,
After which, he proceeded the writing to read.
Although the words each had a meaning of their own,
In every one plainly the king's downfall was shown.

The last word written, Daniel said, signified,
The Medes and the Persians should his kingdom divide.
Now Daniel in elegant scarlet robes was arrayed,
And also third ruler, over the kingdom was made.
But that very same night, Belshazzar was slain,
And Darius, the Median, did in his place reign.
Who perceiving the wisdom Daniel possessed,
Promoted him as ruler above all the rest.

Now with jealousy intense, the princes are filled,
Therefore seek every way to get Daniel killed;
But no fault in him do they find in any way,
Except they can make it appear wrong to pray;
So they ask of the king, to send forth this decree,
Every petition, for thirty days, shall be made unto me.
'Twas added, whoever, this command shall disobey,
Then into the lion's den shall be cast right away.

Now the Medes and the Persians when they establish a fact,
According to law, they must never retract.
So that Daniel would die, by intrigue, it now seemed,
Although of this truth the king never dreamed.
But notwithstanding the decree, Daniel did openly pray,
And was reported to Darius, of course, right away.

Now the king, loving Daniel, was greatly distressed,
And sought in some way his sad fate to arrest.
But these crafty men had accomplished their aim,
And now were determined on executing the same.

So Daniel was into the lions' den thrown,
And over its mouth was placed a great stone.

The king could not sleep, for weeping, that night,
So arose in the morning as soon as 'twas light,
And then, to the den of lions he hasted away;
For he believed the God, unto whom Daniel did pray,
Would deliver his servant, and when he found that he had,
He was not much astonished, but exceedingly glad.

Then Daniel was taken, from out the lions' den,
And into it were cast, these cruel wicked men;
Likewise were thrown in, their children and wives,
And the lions immediately destroyed all their lives.
Then the true and living God was confessed by the king,
And he commanded the people to do the same thing.
Great honors on Daniel did Darius bestow,
And by Cyrus, the Persian, he was prospered also.

Now the prophecies of Jeremiah, and Ezekiel, Daniel read,
So to pray for Jerusalem, he was oftentimes led.
Whose seventy years desolation, was now ended, very near,
When according to prophecy, her restoration would appear.
One evening, when Daniel was engaged in fervent prayer,
Of the presence of an angel, he was made fully aware.

'Twas Gabriel, who assured him that his prayers had been heard,
And that God's mercy now would not long be deferred.
For after seventy weeks, his people would be free,
And the rebuilding of Jerusalem permitted to see.
The angel, in the conversation, spoke prophetically, as it were,
Of things that would many years afterward occur.
The coming of Christ, he does now plainly foreshow,
And the second destruction of Jerusalem also.

Some time after this, we read Daniel passed
Three weeks in humble mourning, and likewise did fast,
And then in a vision, unto him doth appear,
That which causes him at first to tremble with fear.
But the angel consoled him, in kind loving ways,
And furthermore spake concerning his people's latter days.

That Persia by four kings, was to be overthrown,
And Babylon destroyed, was unto Daniel made known;
Also that the Romans would invade all their lands,
But Israel, through Michael, would be delivered from their hands.
Concerning Daniel's death, nothing recorded appears,
But this was B. C. about five hundred and thirty-four years.

JONAH.

We read Jonah the prophet was by the Lord sent
To Nineveh, but rather to Joppa he went,

And then to Tarshish, right away paid his fare,
As he discovered a ship which was soon going there.
Now the city of Nineveh, God's laws did defy,
And so he told Jonah against it to cry.
But Jonah, being tempted, the Lord to disobey,
So thought from his presence to flee far away.

But God in the sea, a great tempest now made,
And the mariners, of destruction, were sorely afraid.
Being prompted to believe that this evil was sent,
To cause one of their number of a sin to repent,
And so they cast lots, and on Jonah it fell,
All regarding himself, and the evil to tell.

Accordingly, when unto their questions he replied,
That from God he had fled, they were well satisfied,
And the cause of the tempest, they also well knew,
Was having on board this disobedient Jew.
Jonah being desirous the passengers to save,
To cast him overboard, permission now gave.

The sailors hesitated, but decided at last
That Jonah must surely into the waters be cast.
Which caused the ship to be saved, and Jonah also,
For God, in this way, his mercy doth show.
A great fish he prepared to swallow Jonah straightway;
Three days, and three nights, within it he lay.
And while there, he prayed, for the remission of sin,
Likewise thanking God, that so kind he had been.

Then God spake unto the fish, and did it command,
To vomit Jonah up out on the dry land;

And then unto Jonah, the second time, spake,
Go thou to Nineveh, a message there take.
So Jonah obeyed, and to the people made known,
Forty days, and this city shall be overthrown.

And now the Ninevites believe, and likewise repent,
So the Lord, being merciful, changed his intent.
Then Jonah was displeased, for surely he thought
The people will say, I have falsely them taught.
So God his inconsistency desiring to show,
Caused a great gourd to spring up and grow,
Which, from the sun's heat sheltered Jonah by day,
Also its thick branches kept the dew all away.

Jonah having withdrawn, from the city to grieve,
Was exceedingly glad, this protection to receive.
But it only remained for a day and a night,
When a worm at its roots caused it to blight.
Now the sun beating down, so hot on his head,
Forced Jonah to say, Oh that I were dead.

Then God reprovingly, thus unto him spake,
Should I not compassion on Nineveh take.
And spare the people of that flourishing city,
When thou hast seen fit on the gourd to take pity.
How long after this Jonah was permitted to live,
The Bible, it seems, no record doth give.
In the days of Amaziah he was led to prophesy,
And we find his father was called Amittai:

Books of Prophecy.

To the Books confined to prophecy now we have come,
Of Isaiah and Jeremiah we have already written
    some.

To prophesy in Babylon, Ezekiel began,
Being taken there a captive, when a very young man,
Among the three thousand Nebuchadnezzar carried away,
While others with the king he did ruthlessly slay.

If carefully and patiently, my readers will look
The Old Testammet through, in each following book,
You will find that these prophets foretold Jerusalem's downfall,
And the captivity of Judah, in some way, nearly all.
For the sin of idolatry, they were burdened and grieved,
But that God would be merciful they also believed

Isaiah, Jeremiah, Zechariah, Daniel and Micah did foresee
The coming of Christ, the world to redeem and set free.
By Isaiah was foretold his sufferings and grief,
He likewise predicted the world's rejection and unbelief.
That the temple would be rebuilt, and Jerusalem also,
By the help of King Cyrus, Jeremiah did show.

And we learn these Bible truths did unto him appear
Before coming to pass, one hundred years, very near.
Isaiah told the same about forty years before,
That they both were inspired, do we need proof any more?

If so, for assistance, unto God we must pray,
Who freely will take our unbelief all away.

[*End of the Old Testament.*]

THE NEW TESTAMENT.

THE FOUR GOSPELS COMBINED.

As the rose from the bud does beautifully unfold,
So does the New Testament follow the old.
As the prophets foretold that a Messiah should appear,
So the Gospels proclaim that a Saviour is here.
As for Adam's disobedience the curse, then, God gave,
He also sent Jesus the whole world to save.

And although, after Malachi, no prophetic word,
For four hundred years, the children of men heard,
Then a voice in the wilderness plainly doth say,
For the Lord and his kingdom prepare ye the way.
So we learn, John the Baptist was a messenger by God sent,
To tell of Christ's mission, also warn sinners to repent,
Indeed, the birth of John, and Jesus the same,
The Angel Gabriel was sent to proclaim.

John, the son of Zacharias, early in life did begin
To preach baptism, and the repentance of sin.
Elizabeth, his mother, was for piety noted,
While his father, to the priesthood his life had devoted.
Now the mother of Christ was to Elizabeth a friend,
Being cousins, they both from king David descend.

Thus was it fulfilled, what had been prophesied,
That Shiloh unto Judah should be allied.
But although the Virgin Mary was unto Jesus a Mother,
His father was God, and all of God's children Christ's brothers.
For 'tis the promise, that all who believe on His word
This honor upon them shall then be conferred.

Of Christ's birth and life, his crucifixion and ascension,
According to the Gospels we now shall make mention:
But if the dear loving Saviour, we would personally know,
Of him we must learn and accept him also.
Now Joseph, the carpenter, made Christ's mother his wife,
For an angel had told him concerning her life,
That by the Holy Ghost, the child Jesus was conceived,
And so in Mary's purity, he fully believed.

Soon after, Joseph and Mary from Nazareth went,
To transact business in Bethlehem being their intent.
It would seem that the people, by a ruler's decree
Were all taxed, and in their own city should be:
So Joseph and Mary, now to Bethlehem must go,
Their relation to the house of David to show;
And then was fulfilled, what Micah did declare,
For Jesus was born while Joseph and Mary were there.

The Inns being full, there seemed no other way
Than some should sleep in out-buildings on hay.
Now Joseph and Mary had such a bed made,
And Jesus, when born, in a manger was laid.
Notwithstanding, God's glory around the babe shone;
While angels rejoiced the good tidings to make known.
But not to the rich, the mighty, or great,
Did God's Holy messengers their story relate.

'Twas unto the shepherds the angel did say,
In Bethlehem is born a Saviour to-day.
We read a great multitude of angels came then,
Shouting peace on earth, and good will toward men;
And that when these Holy messengers for Heaven departed,
To find Jesus the shepherds immediately started.
And the babe was found, as the angels had said,
In a manger, which served in the place of a bed.

And so the whole truth the shepherds having learned,
Praising God for the gift, unto their flocks then returned.
The eighth day, the child for circumcision was brought
To a priest, for thus the Jews were all taught.
But this precious babe had already been named
By Gabriel, at the time his birth was proclaimed.

And then Jesus, when Mary's purification expired,
Was taken to the temple, for so the law required.
Every mother at this time a sacrifice should make;
A pair of turtle doves, the poorest all take :

That Mary and Joseph were poor, we now readily see,
As a pair of these doves was Mary's offering to be.

Before leaving the temple, two holy people came,
The divinity of Jesus prophetically to proclaim.
Although at this time he was only forty days old,
The glad news of his birth far and near had been told.
For we learn wise men living in the East, then afar,
Came to worship the child, being guided by a star.

Now when Herod the king these wonderful things heard,
To the priests and the scribes he immediately sent word.
Then concerning the prophecies of Christ, he inquired,
For to learn the truth of the matter, he greatly desired.
And if this young child, was to him disenthrone,
Some way to destroy him he then would make known.

What he learned of the prophecies, greatly distracted his mind ;
So he sent wise men the child Jesus to find.
Who soon saw the babe, for the star did them guide ;
But unto the king was this privilege denied.
For a message God sent to these men when asleep,
The situation of the child from king Herod to keep ;
And warned Joseph to flee into Egypt, straightway
For Herod was seeking the young child to slay.

So he went as directed, and there did abide
With the child and its mother until king Herod died.
Herod anxiously waited for the wise men to return,
But that they have departed he doth soon after learn;

And so if this babe he purposed to slay,
He must now resort to some other way.

Of Joseph's flight into Egypt he had no intimation,
And so he now ordered the immediate extermination
Of every male child, aged two years or less,
That the people in his realm far or near did possess.
Accordingly great numbers of innocent children were killed,
And thereby a prophecy of Jeremiah's was fulfilled;
But this thing to Herod no great pleasure doth give,
For only a short time is he permitted to live.

And so out of Egypt God now called his Son;
As Hosea had prophesied, thus so was it done.
Now Joseph into Jerusalem would have immediately returned,
But that Archelaus was king on his journey he learned.
And that *he*, like his father, a wicked life led,
Therefore he decided to go to Nazareth instead.

Now each day added strength to the child did impart,
And God's grace abounded also in his heart.
For we read that when Jesus was twelve years of age,
In a conversation with the doctors he did understandingly engage.
'Twas in the temple, which his parents had ever held dear,
And to keep the feast of the passover went every year.

Returning this time, they had journeyed a whole day,
When they learned Jesus behind them in the temple
　　did stay:
So they turned back to Jerusalem, and there Jesus
　　found,
With the doctors of divinity, seeking the scriptures
　　to expound.
When talking with his mother, he was fain to avow
The business of his father he must be about now.
Joseph and Mary were unable the child to under-
　　stand,
But as he was wont to obey their every command,
He now unto Nazareth with them returned;
And of his attributes divine all afterwards learned.

To baptize him recorded in the Gospels we find,
Was unto John the Baptist the pleasant duty
　　assigned;
Who although to the ministry had early been led,
To be baptized of Jesus he requested instead.
But Jesus, to teach our Heavenly Father's will,
Said suffer it so now, all righteousness to fulfil.

Then a blessing followed, as soon as 'twas done,
For God acknowledged Jesus as his well-beloved son.
In whom I am well pleased, he added also,
The importance of obedience thus he plainly doth
　　show.
But the blessing which was precious all others above,
Was the gift of the Holy Spirit, in the form of a dove.
This God permitted his beloved son to see,
While in the Heavens there appeared an opening to be.

Now God and his Son together had planned,
That the infirmities of man he should fully understand.
And that from temptation he should not be exempt,
So he was led into the wilderness for Satan to tempt.
After fasting forty days, the tempter then said,
If God's son, now command that these stones be made bread.
But this answer did Jesus then unto him give,
Not on bread alone, but by God's word, shall man live.

Then unto a high pinnacle of the temple being led,
Cast thyself down, Satan wickedly said.
To rebuke him, then Jesus this hastened to say,
To tempt the Lord God is to him disobey:
Then the devil to tempt him, the third time did try,
After taking him up into a mountain very high,
If thou wilt fall down, said he, and worship me,
All the kingdoms of the world I will give unto thee.

But the holiness of Christ was ever his defense,
And he now commanded Satan that he should go hence.
For 'twas written, and thereby plainly made known,
That God we must serve and him worship alone.
Thus Satan was vanquished, and from Jesus he fled,
And God's Holy angels ministered unto him instead.

Now during Christ's absence we find John had been preaching,
Of the coming Messiah, whose greatness he was teaching.

So to learn about Christ, the Jews now desire,
And they send priests and Levites, of John to inquire
If John were not Christ. The Pharisees thought,
Why should he baptize, and had he really ought?
He said, 'tis with water, thus repentance to show,
But only through Christ can you the Holy Ghost know.

Soon after this, Jesus, near the Jordan did appear,
Behold now said John is the Lamb of God here.
He also bare record of all that was done
When Jesus was baptized, and owned as God's son.
Thus several became Christ's disciples straightway,
For on him they believed, and him desired to obey.

And now the first miracle by Jesus was wrought,
It seems wine at a wedding was a necessity thought.
So at a marriage in Cana, there being none,
To make wine from pure water by Jesus was done.
But where 'twas procured, only the servants there knew,
Who filled the vessels with water, and then the wine drew;
Still the ruler of the feast, when tasting the wine,
To the bridegroom pronounced it to be very fine.

Then Jesus, his mother, and four disciples also,
Soon after the wedding, to Capernaum go;
After staying a few days, then to Jerusalem Jesus went,
To celebrate the passover being his intent;
When he found in the temple, doves, oxen and sheep,
Brought there by their owners, a benefit to reap.

Also changers of money he found sitting about,
But with a scourge of small cords he drove them all out;
And then in the future he forbade them, likewise,
Of making his Father's house one of merchandise.

The Jews now seemed to be deeply impressed,
That some hidden power was by Jesus possessed.
And so they requested some sign he would show,
That his superiority was valid, thus they might know;
Said Jesus, if the temple were destroyed, I would raise
It most surely again, unto you, in three days.

The temple now standing, so in history we read,
Was reared by king Herod, as chief man to lead.
And in the building of which, forty-six years it did take,
But Jesus of the temple of his body then spake.
Which the disciples remembered, when he was risen from the dead,
And they accordingly believed every word he had said.

We know not how long Jesus in Jerusalem now stayed,
But that while remaining there many converts he made;
Among those who found the way to salvation and light
Was Nicodemus, a ruler, who came to Jesus by night.
To question the Master, this Pharisee was made bold,
Who unto him, accordingly, many precious truths told.

That God must be with him, Nicodemus surely thought,
Because of the wonderful miracles he had wrought.

But Jesus, when answering, said unto him then,
None can enter God's kingdom, except born again.
The second birth, to Nicodemus, was a great revelation,
But he learned it was spiritual, and led to Salvation,
And it seems God's kingdom he did then anxiously seek,
For Jesus was led thus of the sacrifice to speak.

As the serpent was lifted up, so is God's son to be,
That whosoever believeth shall eternal life see;
For God so loving the world, his only son gave,
That the perishing, by believing on him he might save.
Thus works without faith, Jesus made very plain,
To secure life eternal, would be done only in vain;
These truths on Nicodemus a profound impression made,
For to openly confess Jesus he was never after afraid.

Now Jesus and his disciples into the country soon go,
And we read John was baptizing in Enon also.
And that most of his converts were jealously inclined,
Because Jesus was baptizing great numbers, they find.
But John took occasion to bear a final testimony now,
For Christ's great superiority he did humbly allow.

He also made known, if God's son was denied,
His wrath on all such would forever abide;
For God loved his Son, and by his command,
Every thing was delivered, now into his hand
To avoid farther trouble, John the baptist soon went
To Galilee, where his preaching caused many to repent.

And so the ruler of Judea, Herod Antipas by name,
Went out to hear John, because of his fame.

Herod at this time, was with his brother's wife living,
And great occasion for scandal he thereby was giving;
So John to rebuke him, unto him said,
Unlawfully, thou hast thy brother's wife wed.

Then Herodias insisted this sentence should be passed,
That John into prison should be immediately cast,
And had the king followed the advice of his wife,
John the baptist, no doubt, would have then lost his life;
But Herod, although at the time was quite wroth,
To destroy him entirely he also was loth.

And now a feast being made, on the king's birthday,
The daughter of Herodias entertained him this way,
By dancing before him, with such grace and ease,
That both he and his guests she highly doth please.
Therefore unto the damsel, king Herod did say,
Ask what thou wilt, and it shall be given straightway

So she consulted her mother, who unto her said,
Go ask of the king, to give you John's head.
The king was sore grieved, but his oath having given,
To order John beheaded, he felt he was driven.
Thus the head in a charger, was unto Salome sent,
Who with it to her mother immediately went.

Now not long after the time John to Galilee came,
Jesus left Judea, and went there the same.
Traveling through Samaria, he came to Jacob's well;
Being weary with his journey, he stopped there a spell.
His disciples, however, to the city of Sychar went,
To purchase some provisions being then their intent.

While resting by the well, Jesus there a woman saw,
A Samaritan, thought Jesus, she will some water draw,
And so he being thirsty, asked the woman for a drink,
Who perceiving 'twas a Jew of this doth strangely think.
The Jews and the Samaritans are at enmity she said,
But to reveal himself unto her, it seems, was Jesus led.

Said Jesus, if thou knewest, who asked to drink of thee,
Living water I would give, for you'd ask it then of me,
The woman being puzzled, Jesus said unto her then,
He who drinketh of this water, shall surely thirst again.
But that which I will give, from thirst will make you free,
And unto everlasting life will a well of water be.

Then Jesus told her truly relating to her life,
Unto husbands five, already, she had been a wife.
That Jesus was a prophet, the woman surely thought,
And so the place of worship, before him now she brought;
Instead of in Jerusalem, the Samaritans had made
A temple on Mount Gerizim, and there their reverence paid.

Then Jesus told her plainly, all worship to be real,
Within, God's Holy Spirit every one must truly feel.
Said she, Messias cometh, that this is true I know,
And then all things mysterious to us he'll plainly show.
Now Jesus unto her declared himself the Christ to be,
When his disciples coming, strangely thought these things to see.
So the woman did not tarry any longer at the well,
But departed for the city, of the Messiah there to tell.

Thus a great many Samaritans of Jesus Christ now heard,
And many were converted, because to them he preached God's word;
Thereby Jesus taught a lesson, that no preference he gave,
But the lost of every station, all alike he came to save
Two days in Samaria, this time, he only stayed,
And then to Galilee, his journey quickly made.
The Galileans now were ready the Lord Jesus to receive,
For being at the passover, they on his power believe.

Now a nobleman in Cana, came unto him to say,
At Capernaum my son sick unto death doth lay.
That he could heal and save him, the nobleman felt sure,
And so he importuned him, his son to go and cure,

Thy son doth live, said Jesus, which afterwards he knew,
And all of Jesus' sayings proved likewise to be true.
So he, and his whole family believed on Jesus' name,
And many more in Cana his followers became.

But now the steps of Jesus to Nazareth were turned;
For his childhood's home to visit he oftentimes had yearned.
And by the Holy Spirit, while there, was Jesus led,
Yet, 'tis the son of Joseph, the people doubting said.
Then verily, said Jesus, I now say unto you,
In his own land, no prophet is accepted to be true.

Other truths he uttered, which did with wrath them fill,
And so they thrust him out, intending him to kill.
But it was not so ordered that Jesus now should die,
And so into Capernaum, he passed them safely by.
Here, by the Sea of Galilee, did Jesus preach and pray,
While many unclean spirits he likewise drove away.

The sick and the afflicted were unto him all brought,
To stay with them continuous the people him besought.
Indeed, so many came, his precious truths to hear,
That Simon's ship he entered, to preach, it doth appear.
Within the ship was Simon, and Andrew too, his brother,
While James and John quite closely by do occupy another.

We read these fishermen had all night toiled in vain,
But Jesus after preaching, did unto them make plain;
That he their every burden would surely help to bear,
If him they'd follow wholly, and in his labors share.
For with a draught of fishes he filled their ships and then—
Said follow me, and henceforth be fishers after men:
So Simon, Andrew, James and John, the sons of Zebedee,
True followers of Jesus proclaimed themselves to be.

And now the fame of Jesus throughout Judea spread,
For his miracles were wonderful, even raising of the dead;
But in all of Jesus' work, he made it manifest,
That faith was a prerequisite when asking to be blest.
'Twas not for fame, nor riches, Jesus' miracles were done,
But to glorify the Father, he did them every one.

And he was also constant, to teach, to preach, and heal,
And yet, sometimes exhausted, he could not help but feel;
But the sick and the afflicted did so besiege him now,
That not a moment's rest they unto him allow;
And so we read it happened upon a certain day,
Returning from the wilderness, where he had been to pray,

Great multitudes had gathered, his precious truths to hear,
Among them Scribes and Pharisees, who only came to sneer

But an opportunity soon offered Jesus' power to demonstrate;
A helpless paralytic, whose faith was very great,
Was to him brought by friends, while on his bed he lay,
However, for the multitude, he must have gone away,
Had they not persevered, and on the housetop went,
While there to make an opening their energies were bent,
Then through the tiling down, this palsied man they lower,
Until in front of Jesus his bed rests on the floor.

Great faith this man possessed, could Jesus plainly see,
And so said he, thy sins now are forgiven thee.
Said the Pharisees and Scribes, sin, God forgives alone,
So Jesus then his potency to them made plainly known.
Then unto the paralytic, again, he kindly said,
Arise, go to thy house, and with thee take thy bed.
The man departed well and strong, and so he did thereby,
Amaze the people, who were led the Lord to glorify.

Next Jesus met a publican, Levi, we find his name,
Who unto him a follower, right there and then became.

Now both publicans and Gentiles quite oft with Jesus meet,
And often, all together, they likewise sit to eat.
But that it is a sin, the Scribes and Pharisees all think,
For Jesus thus with sinners, to freely eat and drink.
I came to call, said Jesus, the sinners to repent,
And not to call the righteous have I to earth been sent.

But so envious of Jesus, are these self-righteous men,
They seek for an occasion to find fault with him again.
And so when his disciples, upon the Sabbath day,
Plucked corn to eat, these men were very quick to say,
It surely is not lawful, for thy disciples to do so.
Then Jesus using Scripture, unto them did plainly show,
No day are we forbidden to supply our pressing need;
Nor should we e'er refuse to do, a kind or humane deed.
This Jesus by example, made them to understand,
For on that Sabbath day, restored he a withered hand.
But some way to destroy him the Pharisees are bent,
And with the Herodians to counsel, accordingly they went;
But all their plans and purposes did Jesus fully know,
And therefore to Jerusalem he thought it best to go.

But it mattered not to Jesus, unto what place he went,
For his life in doing good was ever wholly spent.
At Bethesda's pool a multitude of helpless, blind and weak,
Had gathered there, their health, and also strength to seek,

And one more helpless far, than any of the rest,
Was selected first by Jesus, to heal, and thus be blessed.
And although thirty-eight years this man has helpless been,
Said Jesus walk, and so he does at once begin.
And as he homeward went the Pharisees he saw,
Who at once to talk with him, began about the law:
Said he, the man that made me whole did also say,
Take up thy bed, although it was the Sabbath day.

And now we learn again, these austere, angry Jews,
With crime deserving death, the Saviour did accuse;
And so our Lord declared that all the works he'd done,
Were through the power of God, imparted to his son;
And that his Heavenly Father had unto this world him sent,
To do these very things, that sinners might repent.

After this, unto a desert place, we learn that Jesus went,
And there a night in humble prayer and solitude he spent,
But in the morning early his work began again,
We read the twelve apostles by him were chosen then.

That they should all co-operate, and labor in his name,
By him it was intended, when his apostles they became.
So they went into the mountain, that Jesus might, while there,
For their high and Holy calling, these chosen ones prepare.

And in this precious sermon, given on the mount, we find
Both the spirit and the law, most beautifully combined.
It was then given to them, it was meant for us all,
And if we follow it, surely, we never shall fall.
Against worshiping, like the Pharisees, he bade them beware;
And so for an example he then gave the Lord's prayer.
To exemplify Christ's teachings, oh, let us all try,
For our dear Father in Heaven we shall then glorify.

A Centurion in Capernaum did Jesus next await,
That he might heal his servant, whose sufferings were great;
But so great was the faith the Centurion possessed,
That Jesus would speak, he did only request.
Then the servant was healed, but said Jesus, indeed
The faith of this man does all others exceed.

The raising of the dead is the miracle next wrought,
The dead son of a widow unto life being brought.
And now a beautiful lesson, we have next to record,
In which a penitent sinner Jesus did richly reward.
While sitting with a Pharisee, at his table to eat,
This woman did kiss and anoint Jesus' feet.

The Pharisee, well knowing her sins to be great,
Thought even her touch would them both 'contaminate;
But Jesus her sins freely forgave, and also,
Told her in peace from them now she might go.
For, said he, her love in the same ratio will be
As her sins, from which she now is set free.

Now Jesus, by miracles had his power mostly shown,
And so he decided some truths to make known,
By using parables, so simple, yet practical and plain,
That in ignorance no longer need any remain.
In the parable of the sower he plainly does show,
That when hearing the word, we must keep it also.
Concerning the kingdom of heaven several parables he spake,
In which their meaning so obvious, no one need mistake;
For these simple illustrations all point in one way,
To a needful preparation for the great judgment day.

Jesus at this time from the multitude to be free,
Was preaching in a vessel, on the Sea of Galilee;
Being weary, at length, he sought some repose,
But only slept a short time when a fierce storm arose;
Indeed, his companions were all filled with fright,
For the wind and the waves were a terrible sight.
Carest thou not that we perish, said they?
But they learned that the winds, even, Jesus obey.
For when to the sea he said, peace, be still!
It was calm and submissive, then, unto his will.

And so they passed safely now over the lake,
Where Jesus of a demoniac a sane man doth make;
A long time this poor man had been without rest,
For by a legion of devils he was wholly possessed.
But Jesus from him did now cast them all out,
Into a large herd of swine, that were feeding about.
Which running into the lake were immediately drowned,
While the miserable demoniac his dear Saviour had found.

But Jesus with the Gadarenes no longer could stay,
And so with his disciples he hastened away,
Back over the sea, where the multitude he found
Awaiting his coming, thus they soon him surround.
First Jairus, a ruler, came and fell at his feet,
And to heal his little daughter did him earnestly entreat.

So Jesus started to go, when a poor woman drew near,
Whose faith was very great, but she also showed fear,
For instead of speaking with the Master, freely to his face,
Behind him she timidly sought out a place,
But that of her disease she would now be relieved,
This poor sufferer surely must have firmly believed.

For although twelve years having doctored in vain,
An issue of blood, which caused her much pain,
If I can but touch his garment she thought,
My permanent cure will be instantly wrought.

Nor was her great faith unrewarded to be,
For as she believed, so was she made free.

Now Jesus of some presence was fully aware,
So he questioned his disciples concerning the affair.
Then the woman tremblingly at his feet fell,
Also the whole truth did unto him tell.
Said Jesus, 'twas faith that secured thy release,
Thou art perfectly whole, so depart thou in peace.

But while he was speaking, unto Jairus 'twas said,
Why trouble the Master? Thy daughter is dead.
Said Jesus, believe, and do not lament;
And then unto the damsel they immediately went
When seeing her, this unto her parents he said,
Thy daughter sleepeth, and is not now dead.
And so it proved true, for she stood on her feet,
When commanded by Jesus, and likewise did eat.

So now Jesus' fame, throughout all Judea spread,
And to send forth the twelve he therefore was led.
For the laborers were few, and the harvest so great,
That he felt it unwise any longer to wait.
And so, two by two, they went forth to preach,
And over unclean spirits he gave power to each.

He also adjured them on God alone to rely,
For their wants and necessities he would surely supply.
Following these instructions, throughout Judea they went—
Healing and preaching, that all should repent.
And now King Herod hearing all about Jesus' fame,
To see and hear for himself quite anxious became.

For said he, 'tis John, now risen from the dead;
Although he well knew that he did him behead.

Now the disciples, to confer with Jesus desired,
And unto a desert place, they therefore retired.
But as soon as became their resting place known,
They were permitted no longer to remain there alone.
And so Jesus compassion took upon them again,
For as sheep without a shepherd, had been all these men.

And now fully realizing their every actual need,
He bade his disciples the whole multitude to feed;
Who thought it impossible to comply with his wishes,
As they only possessed five small loaves, and two fishes.
But Jesus first blessed, then brake the fishes and bread,
And so over five thousand, by them, were then fed;
Twelve baskets of fragments were gathered also,
When they all departed, different places to go.

Jesus told his disciples a ship they could take,
And thus cross over to the other side of the lake.
Then after sending the multitude from him away,
He went into the mountain, alone there to pray.
But a storm soon arising Jesus felt he must be
With his disciples, whom he knew were out over the sea.

So he walked on the waves, and when drawing nigh,
Said unto his disciples, fear not, for 'tis I.
Then said Peter, that we may be sure it is true,
Permit me to come, now on the water to you.

Jesus bade him then come, and so he started out,
But soon began sinking, because of his doubt.
Lord save me, he cried ; who did him thus chide :
Oh thou of little faith ; but saved him beside.

Then immediately the wind ceased, and the disciples every one
Came unto him and said, thou art surely, God's Son.
So now very soon they are safely on land,
And when the power of Jesus the people understand,
The diseased from all parts are unto him brought ;
To touch the hem of his garment, he is only besought :
But according to their faith, so is it unto them done,
And perfectly whole, are made every one.

And now the great multitude, which Jesus had fed,
In seeking for him, were to Capernaum led;
But the cause of their anxiety was to Jesus so plain,
That to talk of their spiritual needs he was fain.
Labor not for the food, which perisheth, he said,
But for that which endureth forever, instead.

Although his true meaning they could not under stand,
This life-renewing food they all eagerly demand.
Himself as the bread of life Jesus then did declare,
And that only believers in everlasting life share ;

Farthermore, him that believeth, and cometh unto me,
From hunger and thirst evermore shall be free.

Because of these statements, the Jews with murmurings said,
Can Joseph's son really be of life the true bread?
Jesus, hearing their doubts, his declarations corroborated,
And that from Heaven he came, then additionally stated:
But not to do his own will on earth was he sent,
For in doing God's will was his life to be spent.

And the will of his Father he made very plain;
Was that all through him, should eternal life gain.
Oh how easy he made it, this boon to receive,
Simply come unto Jesus and on him believe.
And that he will accept us, can there be any doubt,
When he said, him that cometh, I will not cast out;
Indeed Jesus' language is so straightforward and plain,
After hearing, in darkness only the obstinate can remain.

But it seems some disciples did now Jesus leave,
Because being unwilling his spiritual doctrines to receive.

Notwithstanding the twelve now with him all stay,
Jesus knew that ere long one would him betray;
And that for his destruction, he saw now likewise,
The Jews eagerly were seeking, some plan to devise.
So that from their persecutions he might be free,
For a while he decided to remain in Galilee.

But the feast of the tabernacles soon drawing near,
In Jerusalem, Jesus felt then obliged to appear;
So he started, but stopped several times on the way;
At Bethsaida first, although he made a short stay,
He proved to the people he was loving and kind,
By restoring the sight of a man who was blind.

At Cesarea Phillippi, to stop next he was led,
And while there to his disciples the following said:
Whom do men say that I am as they see?
When answered, he added, but what sayeth thee?
Thou art Christ, God's Son, Simon Peter replied,
Although afterward Jesus was by him denied.
But his faith with joy, now Jesus' heart filled,
And he said, on this Rock I will my church build.

Now Jesus began unto his disciples to show,
That he must suffer in Jerusalem, but nevertheless go;
And that he should be killed, and on the third day
Be raised up again, he did unto them say.
Then Peter desiring the life of Jesus to save,
Accordingly unto him this advice gave:

Go not among those who will thy life take.
Said Jesus, my sufferings are for righteousness sake,
And he who of God, a true disciple would be,
Must take up his cross, and then follow after me:
For whosoever his life will lose for *my* sake,
Of life everlasting will thus a certainty make.

Six days after this, by St. Mark we are told,
Peter, James and John did Christ's transfiguration behold:

At the same time unto them, did also appear
Moses and Elias, standing by Jesus very near.
Said Peter, three tabernacles, Lord, we would make;
But a bright cloud came over them, while he yet
    spake,
And then a pleased voice was heard by every one,
Saying, hearken ye unto him, for 'tis my beloved
    Son.
Coming down from the mountain, Jesus unto them
    said,
Tell it not openly, until I am risen from the dead.

And now, a hopeless lunatic was by his father
    brought
To Jesus, who to heal him was earnestly besought.
It seems the nine disciples, by Jesus left behind,
For the child with this disease no remedy could find;
But Jesus knew the father did in his power believe,
And so from his affliction he doth his son relieve.
Now the disciples unto Jesus came privately to say,
Why could not we, also, this evil drive away?
If faith ye did possess, as a grain of mustard seed,
Said Jesus, then impossible would be no pure, good
    deed.

And now to his disciples did Jesus speak again,
Of his betrayal and his death, caused by cruel wicked
    men.
The disciples were sore grieved, but did nothing far-
    ther say,
To keep Jesus from the feast of the tabernacles away;

But realizing that ere long they should be left alone,
Many mysterious things besought they Jesus to
  make known.

In the kingdom of Heaven who the greatest should
  be thought,
Was one of the questions which before him now they
  brought.
The kingdom of Heaven, if you would enter therein,
Said Jesus, like children, you must be without sin;
Therefore the humble and meek, the greatest shall be,
And who receiveth one such, in my name, receiveth
  me.
But far better were it to be drowned in the sea,
Than to offend one of these that believeth on me.

That God doth his children care for and keep,
He made plain by the parable of the lost sheep.
Likewise, this assurance he unto them gave,
That the Son of man came, the lost ones to save.
And if we repent, God will us gladly forgive,
Who desires none shall perish, but all eternally live.

And as God forgives us, so shall we, the same way,
Forgive one another—does Jesus farthermore say.
Seven times shall we forgive? Peter wonderingly
  said,
Seventy times seven, quoth Jesus, instead.
And then a plain parable, he did unto them relate,
The punishment of the uncharitable to illustrate.

Now passing through Samaria, ten lepers they espy,
Oh have mercy upon us, Jesus, Master, they cry;

Show yourselves to the priest, he doth unto them say,
And so all were cleansed, and while all haste to obey,
Only one, a Samaritan, ever came and expressed
His thankfulness to Jesus, or ownéd they were blest..

But a profitable lesson to the disciples was taught,
That the good of the whole world by Jesus was sought;
And although his enemies were setting snares for his feet,
His time had not come, nor his work yet complete.
And so, nearing Jerusalem, it seemed only discreet
That Jesus should avoid with very many to meet:
But at the feast of the tabernacles he had nothing to fear,
For so many of his friends were unto him near.
And here a wise discourse Jesus unto them gave,
Assuring believers that he would them all save.

And now among them arose contentions and strife,
For some, had they dared, would have taken Jesus' life.
But the officers that were sent the dear Lord to take,
Confessed that no man like him ever spake.
Nicodemus, the pharisee, no longer any fearing,
Declared it unlawful to judge without hearing.
And although Jesus' enemies dare not now him molest,
They had no intention of letting the matter rest.

But now a certain lawyer, to ask Jesus was fain,
What he should do, eternal life to attain.

Jesus answering the question, unto him said,
Concerning the law, tell me what have you read?
Love God with thy heart, strength, soul and mind,
And thy neighbor as thyself, is commanded, I find.
'Tis right, said Jesus; but the lawyer replied,
Who is my neighbor? that he might be justified.

But Jesus by a parable made it so plain,
That the lawyer in ignorance could no longer remain.
'Twas the good Samaritan, who came to the relief
Of the man that was robbed and wounded by the thief,
Although both a priest and a Levite passed by,
Leaving the man, as they thought, there to die.
And thus the Samaritan, very plainly did show,
That they who love God love his children also.

Now Jesus from Jerusalem to Bethany went,
And a short time with Martha and Mary there spent.
These sisters to Jesus their respects then both pay,
But mark you, how entirely different the way:
Martha was engaged, preparing food for him to eat,
While Mary was delighted to sit at his feet.

And so Martha, feeling her sister to blame,
With complaints unto Jesus accordingly came.
But Jesus, well knowing the desire of Mary's heart,
Assured Martha she had chosen by far the better part.
Oh! how oft did the Father, through his son speak,
That his kingdom first we should every one seek.

Jesus' work at this time, being extensive indeed,
Of more helpers he felt he was greatly in need;
So he appointed seventy, with instructions the same
As given to the twelve, when his apostles they became.

It seems Jesus after this, in the temple again taught,
And while there, the Pharisees unto him brought
A woman, who the seventh commandment had violated;
The punishment was stoning, as by Moses designated:
But the Pharisees, hoping Jesus now to accuse,
Concerning her punishment, asked for his views.

Let him without sin at her cast the first stone,
Said Jesus, who was left with the woman then alone.
For her accusers being caught now in their own snare,
To proceed any farther did not one of them dare.
So the woman uncondemned, then went on her way,
But go and sin no more, Jesus kindly doth say.

Now although he had enemies, many on him believed,
While many were the blessings from him daily received.
Poor Bartimeus, born blind, first saw the light,
When Jesus, on the Sabbath, restored his eyesight.
The Jews ever ready to convict Jesus of sin,
To question Bartimeus right away then begin;

But the cause of the Saviour he was bold to advocate,
And that he must be of God, did unto them state.

For whereas I was blind, now I can see;
And 'twas Jesus, who gave this light unto me.
To cast him out of the city, the Jews now proceed,
But no harm could befall him, with Jesus to lead.
Who not only restored the sight of his eyes,
But unto Salvation he too, made him wise.

While walking on the porch of Solomon one day,
Some half believing Jews unto Jesus did say:
If thou art the Christ, let us plainly so see,
Said he 'tis my works that bear witness of me.
Then the parable of the good shepherd he unto them gave,
Telling them plainly his own sheep he would save.

That he was the door of the sheepfold, he said,
Also the Good Shepherd by whom they were led;
And that if by him any should enter therein,
They then are made free from the bondage of sin.
But he that entereth not in by the door,
A thief and a robber surely is, and no more.

Believers he represented, to be his own sheep,
Given by the Father for him safely to keep;
Also his own life he said he should give,
That his followers, through him, might eternally live.
He told them that he and the Father were one,
But that through his Father the works were all done.

Then to stone him attempted the incredulous Jews,
While of blasphemy also they did him accuse.
Now Jesus lovingly tried to make them understand,
But was obliged for safety to escape from their hand.
And soon beyond Jordan we find him again,
Devoting his time to the salvation of men.

While there this sad news was unto him brought;
That Lazarus was dying, by his sisters was thought,
His sisters were Martha and Mary the same,
Who to anoint Jesus' feet unto him came.
That the coming of Jesus would Lazarus relieve,
Mary and Martha did most truly believe;
And although to Bethany Jesus intended to go,
He purposely delayed, God's glory to show.

But soon after starting to his disciples he said,
Lazarus I must raise, for he is already dead.
Martha, meeting the Saviour, by her conversation proved
That her faith in his power still was unmoved.
Thy brother shall rise again, Jesus doth say,
She answering said, at the resurrection day.

The resurrection and life, said Jesus, am *I*,
And he who believeth in me shall never die:
Then Martha confessed him the true Messiah to be
And went for her sister, the Master to see.
As Martha's faith also was Mary's the same,
But weeping, with very many others she came.

The Lord Jesus Divine, but human likewise,
Tearfully with these mourners did now symphathize.

And so to the grave he asked to be shown,
Also requested they should take away the stone
Four days my brother has already been dead;
It seems, rather doubtingly, by Martha was said.
But Jesus replied, if thou believest in me,
The glory of God, I have said, thou shalt see.
So after thanking his Father, with a loud voice he cried,
Come forth unto him who had sickened and died.
Then Lazarus, bound, hand and foot, in grave clothes,
From out of his sepulcher, immediately uprose.

And so, many of the Jews on Jesus believed,
For that God was with him they plainly perceived.
But his enemies declare, something now must be done,
For ere long on Jesus would believe every one.
And then the Romans, believing him, also, to be king,
Cæsar their nation into subjection would bring

Now Caiphas, the high priest, came forward to say,
To put Jesus to death would be far the best way,
Therefore Jesus to Ephraim, near the wilderness did go,
For of their wicked intentions he was permitted to know.
But not long in seclusion did he purpose to stay,
For his work was unfinished, and he must not delay,
So toward the city of Jerusalem he again started out,
Preaching at the places which lay in his route.
And we find in parables, Jesus now mostly spake,
With illustrations so plain that none could mistake.

Talking with a Pharisee, who to believe was inclined,
His position in this way was by Jesus defined ;
A certain man, on a time, a great supper having made,
All tried their invitations in some way to evade.
So he ordered his servant to go out in the street,
And invite every one, he chanced there to meet.

But particularly he desired his servant to find,
The poor, the maimed, the halt and the blind.
Then finding at the table there were vacancies still,
From the highways and hedges he did his room fill.
But those who excused themselves, he firmly declared,
Should not taste the good things that he had prepared.
The first he invited, I suppose, meant the Jews,
And the supper, the Gospel, which so many refuse.

But to find fault with Jesus, again the people begin,
Because he discourses in private, with those addicted to sin ;
Said Jesus, if a large flock of sheep you possessed,
Losing one, you surely would leave all the rest ;
Feeling your work to be imperfectly done,
Until you had found and restored the lost one.

Then Jesus, his meaning more plainly to illustrate,
The parable of the prodigal son doth relate.
Receiving his portion, this son from home went,
And in riotous living, the whole of it spent;
Of the necessaries of life, so great was his need,
That upon the husks of the swine he had purposed to feed.

But thinking of home, with plenty and to spare,
He said, I will arise and in penitence go there.

His unworthiness as a son he now plainly could see,
And so a hired servant he said I will be.
But his father came out, him afar off to meet,
And with the greatest affection doth his son greet.
When reaching his home, he ordered him dressed
In a robe he considered one of the best.
And then after putting some shoes on his feet,
They went to make merry and the fatted calf eat.

But when the elder son all this merriment heard,
His bosom with anger, and jealousy was stirred;
For he declared his father he had ever obeyed,
And yet for his sake, no feast had been made.
Let us together rejoice, the father then said,
For thy brother is alive, who was before to us dead.

He was lost, and is found, but not so with thee,
For thou, my dear son, hast been ever with me.
His restoration can never, thee in any way wrong,
For all that I have unto thee doth belong.
And so great rejoicing, in Heaven there'll be,
Over one repentant sinner, we plainly can see.

And now again Jesus, by a parable taught,
That earthly treasures in Heaven were counted as naught.
For the rich man in torment, to Lazarus cried,
Who at his own gate, a poor beggar had died.
But now in Abraham's bosom, in Paradise laid,
This touching appeal, was unto him made.

For a drop of water, the sufferings to relieve,
Of him whom in life, only good things did receive.

Said Abraham, the gulf between is so wide,
That to cross is impossible, e'en though we tried.
Then he, who had a wicked and wasted life spent,
Entreated that Lazarus to his five brothers be sent,
To warn them to repent, and escape surely thereby
This torment, prepared for the wicked when they die
If they believe not the prophets, then Abraham said,
Neither will they believe, though one arose from the dead.

And now a wealthy young man came forth to beseech,
The way of life eternal, that Jesus would teach.
Said Jesus, the commandments were made to obey;
But them all have I kept, this young man doth say.
Now thy earthly possessions, said Jesus, must be
Distributed to the poor, and then follow me.
The young man, being sorrowful, showed plainly thereby,
'Twas easier for a camel to go through a needle's eye,
Than for any human being, God's kingdom to enter,
Whose affections on riches were permitted to center.

And now little children to Jesus were brought,
But that it was wrong, the disciples all thought:
Said Jesus, suffer them to come unto me,
For of such, the kingdom of Heaven is to be.
The kingdom of Heaven, Jesus also did say,
Is like a householder, hiring laborers by the day.

Although at different hours these workmen began,
The master paid a penny unto each and every man.

Notwithstanding the first, on this price all agree,
No justice in the plan could they readily see;
For if those at the last hour have a penny they say,
We should have more, that bare the heat of the day.
But the parable was given, God's mercy to show,
And that Jesus pays freely the debt we all owe.
If we accept his conditions, and on him believe,
Life everlasting we shall surely receive.

Jesus likewise, unto his disciples did say,
Men ought never to faint, but always to pray.
But if we expect God will our prayers hear,
Self righteous, like the Pharisee, we must not appear.
But rather like the poor publican, let us begin
To pray for God's mercy, and the remission of sin;
For he that is humble, exalted shall be,
Also the self righteous their abasement must see.

Now a publican in Jericho, Zaccheus by name,
To see Jesus, we learn, so anxious became,
That when passing that way, he climbed in a tree,
And thus he was permitted the Saviour to see.
The crowd being great, and he a short man,
Was the cause of his adopting this very wise plan.

Then Jesus perceiving Zaccheus, doth unto him say,
I must abide in thy house, there with thee to-day.
But the people in anger, now with Jesus fault find,
That he unto a sinner is so gracious and kind;

But Zaccheus his faults to Jesus confessed,
And with forgiveness and salvation was immediately blessed.

Then Jesus leaving Jericho, met by the wayside
Two blind beggars, who for mercy unto him cried.
Rebuked by the people, they still louder cry,
When perceiving their faith. Jesus restored them thereby;
Now nearing Jerusalem, Jesus seemed to think best,
At the mount called Olives, to take a short rest.
And that it might be fulfilled, as had been prophesied,
Into Jerusalem meekly on a beast he should ride;
He instructed two disciples how they should proceed,
To find the animal and colt which now he did need.

And so riding into Jerusalem, the multitude by his side,
Hosanna in the highest was exultingly cried.
Indeed, so great were the rejoicings and praise,
That some of the Pharisees objections did raise.
If these should hold their peace, Jesus rebukingly said,
The very stones would cry out, with praises instead.

Although multitudes of followers Jesus now had,
The fate of Jerusalem made him feel very sad:
For to utterly destroy it was now God's decree;
To punish his persecutors, he plainly could see.
And so the way of salvation desiring to teach,
In the temple daily he continued to preach.

Oh how strangely to the converted, doth it appear,
That any could doubt, whom the Savior did hear.
But as it was then, so is it to-day,
All desire to be saved, but in some other way.
And so many from Jesus, the dear Saviour, will turn,
But alas, the penalty they must finally learn—
For everlasting punishment shall the wicked receive,
But life eternal, all those who on Jesus believe.

And although Jesus' followers the temple now fill,
Yet his enemies are plotting, that him they might kill.
In the parable of the vineyard, how plainly 'tis shown,
That their evil intentions were to Jesus well known
The owner of the vineyard, at a certain time, sent
His servants, to collect of the husbandman the rent,
Who not only refused the servants to pay,
But by beating, and stoning, they drove them away.

Then the owner sent forth his *own* son at the last;
Who was slain, and also from the vineyard was cast.
Said Jesus, what think ye by the owner should be done,
To repay these wicked men for killing his son.
That they should be utterly destroyed, his hearers all thought;
Thus a practical lesson was unto them taught.
For that the landlord was God, they very well knew,
And Jesus his son, whom the husbandmen slew.

Now the Pharisees and Saducees with questions Jesus ply,
Thinking to tempt and entangle him thereby:

The Saducees silenced, a lawyer of the Pharisees saw,
So asked which was the greatest command in the law:
Jesus readily answered that the commandment was love,
Which was given and placed all others above.
Now after this time, no more such questions were heard,
For no man was able to answer him a word.

While preaching, Jesus saw, in the temple one day,
The rich with their gifts, made quite a display;
But the widow who seemed so poor and so sad,
Only gave two mites, being all that she had.
Said Jesus, the poor widow more than all is now giving,
For the penny is taken from out of her living.
Whereas, the wealthy, no sacrifice now make,
And therefore a very little credit can take.

To speak of the destruction of the temple now Jesus was fain,
For he knew not one stone would standing remain.
But this prophecy alarmed the disciples very great,
And they sought to ascertain what would be their own fate.
Said Jesus, false prophets and deceivers there will be,
Also pestilence, famine, and wars you will see.

As I have been persecuted, so will ye be the same;
And this will be done for the sake of my name.

But he that unto the end shall endure,
The salvation of God thereby will make sure,
And unto all nations shall the Gospel be taught,
Before ever the world to an end shall be brought.

By the parable of the virgins, he did now illustrate
That to be ready for this day the necsssity was great.
The kingdom of heaven, he said, should be then
Like virgins in number amounting to ten,
Who, to meet the bridegroom, went out every one,
But five were foolish, and did this risk run.

Although they knew not how long they might tarry,
No extra oil for their lamps do any of them carry.
And so, at midnight, their lights burning low,
To borrow of the wise, the foolish then go;
But they having kept their own lamps in repair,
No oil had they now they could very well spare.

And so to buy oil these five foolish ones went,
But were left in the end their folly to lament,
For the wise ones to the Feast with the bridegroom
    all go,
While the foolish, when coming, he did not even know,
And although for admittance, they unto him cried,
The door he had closed and farther entrance denied.

In the parable of the talents, likewise Jesus doth show,
That the humblest and weakest a duty unto God owe.
A rich man with his servants, his worldly possessions
    leave,
But expects from each one, some revenue to receive.
As their abilities differed, so did the talents the same,
Accordingly five, two and one, the ratio became.

The five talents were doubled, and so were the two,
But the servant having one, nothing with it did do.
And so the master took his buried talent away,
And gave it to the others, then also did say—
This unprofitable servant, into outer darkness cast ye,
Where weeping and gnashing of teeth there will be.
But the others, who faithfully their time did employ,
With commendations were bidden to enter into the
    Lord's joy.

In the great judgment day, now by Jesus was shown,
Will the son of man come, to sit on his throne,
Then all nations before him, will he divide,
The good from the bad, on an opposite side.
Those on the right hand, he will graciously bless,
For the kingdom of Heaven are they to possess.

But those on the left, forever shall share,
The place which for Satan, God did prepare.
Yet, although he prepared this everlasting fire,
That all shall escape it, is his earnest desire.
And that all might believe, be baptized and repent,
Into this world the Lord Jesus was sent.

But the time was approaching when he must be killed,
For his earthly mission was very nearly fulfilled.
To the palace of the high priest, Caiaphas, by name,
The scribes, priests and elders, for consultations now
    came.
For they plan by subtilty, the dear Lord to take,
And conclude, after the passover, a beginning to make.

Each night unto Bethany did Jesus now retire;
Yet he knew that these men met against him to conspire.
And that Judas Iscariot would him betray,
Into his enemies' hands, at no great distant day.
One evening while Jesus was sitting at meat,
With a very costly ointment, Mary anointed his feet.
But this kind loving act, did Judas Iscariot offend.
That it be sold for the poor, does hypocritically recommend.

Jesus knowing his hypocrisy, did then unto him say,
This ointment she has kept, for my burial day.
Then Judas being angry, to Jesu's enemies went,
For to betray him at once was now his intent.
So for thirty pieces of silver the bargain was made,
And for the close of the passover, they only delayed.

Soon Jesus, and his disciples, at a certain house meet,
The feast of the passover together to eat.
When the feast being ready, then Jesus doth say,
Verily, one of my disciples shall soon me betray:
Then he afterward told them, who it should be,
For Judas was led to say, Master, is it me?

Now Jesus the bread, did both bless and break,
Saying, this is my body, so of it partake.
Giving thanks from the cup, they must drink he too said,
For this is my blood, for the remission of sins shed.
'Tis the fruit of the vine, when I drink it again,
In my own Father's kingdom, I will be with you then.

Now to set an example he washed all their feet,
That they should do likewise, he said it was meet.
For if ye love one another, as I have loved you,
All men will thus know as disciples ye are true.

Then, when of his departure he unto them spake,
Said Peter, my life, I will lay down for thy sake.
The cock shall not crow, Jesus answering said,
Ere three times, to deny me you will be led.
But that his disciples truly for him did grieve,
Jesus was fain, nevertheless, to believe.

For many comforting things he did unto them say,
And that to his Father he for them would pray;
That when he was taken, another comforter he would send,
Who would always be with them, even unto the end.
He told them his departure was all for the best,
For he went to prepare a place for their rest.
Said he, where I am there ye also may be,
I in the Father and ye then in me.

So be ye not troubled, but in me believe,
And whatsoever you ask that will you receive.
For I am the vine, and the branches, are ye,
And so nothing can you do except 'tis through me.
If ye love me, my commandments ye then will obey,
And for blessings in my name unto God you must pray.
When risen from the dead, I will see you again;
Although sorrowful now, we will rejoice together then,

And now Jesus' soul was poured out in prayer,
For his disciples, and the burden, he so soon was to bear;
For the hour having come, he was troubled, and yet
That he came for this cause, he did not forget.
If possible, he prayed, let this cup pass me by;
But Father, thy name thou must now glorify.

Thus the human in his nature only did shrink,
When thinking of the cup of which he must drink.
And his life a sacrifice, he willingly gave,
Thereby the whole world desiring to save.
Oh, how dearly the Lord must love every one,
Thus to give as a ransom his well-beloved son.

But ought Jesus alone this burden to bear,
And we, the transgressors, have in it no share?
'Twas not so intended, we plainly can see,
For Jesus has said, ye must *all* follow me.
And if any deny him, he has said furthermore,
He will also deny them, his Heavenly Father before
But all of our burdens, God will help us to bear,
If, like the dear Saviour, we seek him in prayer.

And now a holy angel unto Jesus was sent,
To strengthen and bless him in the coming event.
But the disciples now sleeping, Jesus doth unto them say,
Lest tempted ye be, now arise up and pray.
But a multitude he beheld, while he yet spake,
And Judas, to kiss him, does now undertake;
But Jesus, rebukingly, did unto him say,
With a kiss, the son of man you would betray.

A servant of the high priest, by the disciples stand-
    ing near,
Peter drew out his sword and cut off his ear.
Jesus, healing the wound, had the sword put away,
Saying, if to the Father for help I should pray,
A Heavenly host you would immediately see:
Yet the scriptures fulfilled, at this time are to be.
But with staves and with swords, why are ye here?
That ye came for a thief, so would it appear.

But now unto the high priest, Jesus was led,
While his disciples in fear, away from him fled.
Only Peter and John followed after we read,
And that John being admitted, did for Peter inter-
    cede.
The portress inquiring, if he was a disciple also,
Then Peter pretended he did not even Jesus know.
Being questioned, three times, he thus Jesus denied,
But wept bitterly, thinking what had been prophe-
    sied.

False witnesses against Jesus, having been sought,
Two into his presence, were accordingly brought:
But these, disagreeing, then Caiaphas began,
For the destruction of Jesus to otherwise plan.
That he shall declare his divinity, now is the scheme,
And then put him to death, as they who blaspheme.

Although quiet and passive, Jesus would not deny,
That he was God's own Son, and so he must die:
Notwithstanding, no fault in him was there found,
Yet to condemn him to death were these wicked
    men bound.

Also the officers struck him, and spat in his face,
Which added still farther to their shame and disgrace.
But the Jews had no power to execute any one,
Being subject to Rome, through them must it be done.

And so now with Jesus, before Pontius Pilate they go,
And that he is a malefactor try vainly to show;
But the innocence of Jesus, Pilate plainly could see,
So sent him to Herod, the governor of Galilee.
Now Herod was glad, because of the thought,
Some miracles by Jesus he would surely see wrought.

But Jesus, one word would not unto him say,
And so mocking and dressing him in gorgeous array,
He is sent back to Pilate, who endeavored again,
To show forth that Jesus they should not condemn;
Then, too, while conversing, came a message from his wife,
Warning him to do nothing to take Jesus' life.

But instead of using his authority as he ought,
Many arguments of justice, before the people he brought.
And then mentioned his custom one prisoner to release,
But this effected nothing in the way of making peace.
For they would not have Jesus, but Barrabas instead,
Who the life of a murderer and robber had led.

But what will you do with Jesus? Pilate replied,
They all readily answered, he shall be crucified.
Then Pilate washed his hands before them and said,
If the blood of this just man now must be shed,

The whole responsibility is yours and not mine;
And so into your hands I now Jesus resign.

It seems, the Roman soldiers, did charge of him take
Likewise, for his head a crown of thorns make;
Also before his crucifixion, by Pilate he was scourged,
Yet continually his justification by him was urged.
And he would have released him, no doubt, in the end,
But was told, by so doing, he was not Cesar's friend.
So the Jews were permitted to carry the day,
And Jesus was sentenced, then led captive away,
While the soldiers were allowed him to shamefully treat,
For, besides mocking and jeering, they also him cruelly beat:
But Judas, repenting, came unto the council to say,
It is innocent blood which I was led to betray.

The thirty pieces of silver, he was for the deed paid,
Before going away in the temple he laid;
And then before Jesus had been crucified,
With bitter remorse, he committed suicide.
To put the silver in the treasury the priests did not dare,
So they purchased a potter's field, and buried strangers there.

A multitude followed Jesus to Calvary we read,
And in it were women, who for mercy did plead.
Said Jesus, weep not, for the day draweth nigh,
When for mountains to fall and cover them they'll cry.

Jesus bearing his cross, with exhaustion soon fell,
And then to carry it, Simon, a Cyrenian they compel.

In every possible way, they seek Jesus to disgrace,
So between two thieves on the cross him they place.
And when they had cruelly nailed him thereto,
Said he Father forgive, they know not what they do.
But the soldiers mocked, and derided to the last,
Also parted his raiment, and for it lots cast.
Pilate wrote on his cross Jesus, king of the Jews;
But the chief priests objected, when they did it peruse,
And wanted it written, Jesus *said so*, instead,
But what I have written I have written, Pilate said.

One of the thieves, on the cross by Jesus' side,
In derision with the Jews, likewise unto him cried;
But the other, his divinity seeming to see,
Said when in thy kingdom Lord, remember thou me.
Verily, said Jesus, I now say unto thee,
To-day in Paradise, with me thou shalt be.

Three Marys, one of them unto Jesus a mother,
The wife of Cleophas, and Mary Magdalene the other,
While standing by the cross, to his mother Jesus spake,
Looking to John, for a son him you'll take.
The third hour we read, was Jesus crucified,
And that 'twas the ninth, when he on the cross died.
From the sixth to the ninth, total darkness was sent,
And the veil of the temple was in the midst rent,
In great agony of mind, now Jesus seemed to be,
For he cried out, my God! why hast thou forsaken me.

I thirst! is the next exclamation they hear,
Then his mouth is moistened with some vinegar near.
And now it is finished, his suffering will soon end,
Said he, Father, my spirit into thy hands I commend.
The death of Jesus was followed by a mighty earthquake,
Which caused immense rocks from their foundations to shake.
Also graves were burst open, and many saints were again
Seen walking about, who had long been dead men.
The soldiers, beholding these wonderful things done,
Said, surely this man was God's belov'd Son.

And now the three bodies must be taken away,
For, following the crucifixion was the Mosaic Sabbath day.
But death on the cross was usually very slow,
So to finish the execution, Pilate's soldiers then go.
By breaking their legs, the two thieves were killed,
But Jesus was dead, and the Scripture fulfilled,
For not one bone was broken, as had been prophesied,
But one of the soldiers, with a spear pierced his side.

A rich man of Arimathea, Joseph by name,
To beg Jesus' body for burial, unto Pilate now came,
Then Nicodemus, who came to Jesus to be taught,
Myrrh and aloes, to anoint the precious Lord brought.
After which the body was wrapped in fine linen and laid
In a sepulcher of rock which Joseph had made,

Also over the opening was rolled a great stone,
By Mary Magdalene and another, these things were all known.

Now the priests and Pharisees came unto Pilate and said:
In three days, said Jesus, he would rise from the dead.
So the sepulcher make sure, and thereby prevent,
The disciples from executing any fraudulent intent.
Ye have a watch, said Pilate, go your own way
So a watch was set, but they did not long stay.
For an angel appeared and rolled away the stone,
Then they fled to Jerusalem and their story made known.

Mary Magdalene, and the mother of James and Salome,
When the Sabbath was past, very early left home,
With sweet spices and linen, Jesus' body to anoint,
But to roll away the stone, seemed a difficult point.
When reaching the sepulcher, very great was their surprise,
For the stone was rolled away, notwithstanding its size.
Then entering the tomb, they saw an angel in white,
Which caused them at first to start back in affright.
But the angel assured them they had nothing to fear,
And that Jesus was risen, and no longer here.

Then go tell his disciples that now in Galilee,
As he told them before, they will there Jesus see.

So they hastened away, but did soon Jesus meet,
And with joy inexpressible fell down at his feet.
Then after the greeting, Jesus made the same request
As the angel, regarding the disciples, had expressed
So to Peter and John they first carried the word,
But the news with incredulity by them was heard.

Nevertheless, to the sepulcher they hastened away,
And found the linen clothes where once the Lord lay.
The news that the Lord Jesus had risen from the dead,
Throughout all Jerusalem very rapidly spread.
Notwithstanding the soldiers had been hired to say
That, while sleeping, Jesus' friends stole the body away.

The mother of Jesus, coming weeping to his tomb,
Saw two angels in white sitting still in the room,
Who perceiving her grief, asked why weepest thou?
She answered, I know not where my Lord lieth now.
Then turning around, another form she perceives,
But that 'tis the gardener she fully believes.
And in answer to his question, regarding her grief,
That he has taken Jesus away expresses her belief.

But when the dear Lord called her softly by name,
Of his presence and identity she conscious became,
And would have embraced him, but Jesus said no,
I have not yet ascended, but desire you to go
And say to my brethren, very soon I shall be,
Where my God, and your God, I shall constantly see.

Now two of the disciples, on this very same day,
While journeying to Emmaus, saw Jesus on the way;
Although freely conversing, it was quite a surprise,
When as Jesus at last they did him recognize.
But he vanished away, and then to Jerusalem they return,
That the other disciples of their visit might learn.
And now while together they freely were talking,
Jesus in their midst they plainly saw walking.

Peace be unto you, were the first words he spake,
But he saw for a spirit they did him now take.
Then said he, behold, it most surely is I,
Flesh and bones, you may touch, and yourselves satfy.
Seeing they still wondered, he asked for some meat,
And then in their presence he of it did eat.
Then told them plainly, must be now exemplified
By them, what he taught before being crucified.
Thomas, being absent, did not see Jesus now,
Nor that he had risen would he ever allow;
Except in his pierced side his hand he could thrust,
And the prints of the nails see likewise he must;
But the doubts of Thomas were soon taken away,
For eight days after, Jesus appeared, and did say,
Unto Thomas, whose position he could well understand,
Reach hither, and into my side put thy hand.
So having Thomas convinced, Jesus spake to them all,
Concerning the holy calling, which upon them must fall.

Awhile after this, at the Sea of Tiberias, we read,
The disciples were fishing, but did not succeed,
So Jesus appearing, after they had spent the whole night;
Advised them to cast their nets now, on the right.
That it was the Lord's work, they very soon saw,
For so full were their nets, they could not them draw;
But dragging them along, they soon reached the land,
Which fortunately happened to be close at hand.

And now Jesus gave them to eat, fish and bread,
After which he interrogatively to Simon Peter said,
More than these my disciples, lovest thou me?
Answered Peter, yea Lord, thou knowest I love thee.
Three times, the question was repeated, and likewise,
Peter in the same way made his replies.

His faithfulness, Jesus did prove by this test,
Therefore to feed his sheep did of him request;
And although by Peter he had thrice been denied,
It is obvious that now he did in him confide.
For the shepherd must be faithful, to care for and keep
Safe within the fold, all the lambs and the sheep.

After the crucifixion, forty days having past,
Jesus met with his disciples, we read, for the last;
It was in Galilee, and a great many were led
To draw near to the place, and hear what he said:

Indeed, five hundred were at that time satisfied
That Jesus was risen, who had been crucified.

He told his disciples, that all power had been given,
To him in the earth, and likewise in Heaven.
This power, in a measure, to them he delegated;
Because their lives now were to God consecrated.
And so shall each and all who on Jesus believe,
Spiritual power from the Father receive;
Who desires the whole world to convert and thus save,
For before his departure, this commission Jesus gave:

Go ye to all nations, the Gospel unto them preach,
And what I have here taught, the same you must teach—
For on these things, wholly, does salvation depend,
And lo, alway I am with you, even unto the end.
But remember, Jerusalem you must not one leave,
Until power from on high, through God, you receive.
After this, as far as Bethany, Jesus led the eleven;
And while invoking a blessing, was carried up into Heaven.

THE ACTS OF THE APOSTLES

We read that while Jesus, to Heaven was being carried,
The apostles for some time about the place tarried,
And, while watching, two angels they plainly discern,
Who said, as Jesus went, so should he return.

And then to Jerusalem straightway they went,
There to await the Holy Spirit being their intent.
An upper room in the temple, for their abode they prepare;
And with one accord continue in supplication and prayer.

Besides the apostles, came one hundred and nine
Whose hearts unto God did likewise incline.
Now Peter, in the temple, to preach daily was led,
And in one of his discourses unto them said:
Since Jesus from among us, Judas' name did erase,
Another must be chosen now in his place;
So praying the Lord Jesus, them to direct,
Joseph and Matthias as candidates they select.
But to determine which one, they proceed to lots cast,
And Matthias the favored one was at the last.

The feast of pentecost was after the ascension ten days,
And the disciples were engaged in thanksgiving and praise,
When suddenly a great noise from Heaven they hear,
As a rushing mighty wind, doth it appear.
Likewise, upon each of them suddenly came
Cloven tongues, which seemed like as a flame.
Thus the Holy Ghost plainly doth himself manifest;
And with it they each, and every one are possessed.

Then as the spirit gave utterance, to talk they began,
Which was in different tongues, to further God's plan.

For devout men of every nation, in Jerusalem did
   dwell,
Who could understand their language now perfectly
   well.
But some to make sport did rather incline,
And declared that these men were filled with new
   wine.
But Peter rebuked them, and then farther spake,
Of the Risen Redeemer, whose life they did take.

And thus to repentance these men being led
What now must we do? to the brethren they said.
Repent and be baptized, said Peter, must be done,
For the remission of sins, in Jesus' name, by every
   one.
The Holy Ghost as a gift, you then will receive;
For the promise is given, unto all who believe.
And so that day were baptized, and added, we read,
Three thousand, who continued in the apostles fel-
   lowship and creed.
Then also together, they did praise God and pray,
And believers were added to the church every day.

Now Peter and John, going to the temple to pray,
At the beautiful gate, saw a lame man there lay,
Who a cripple from birth, could no other way live,
Only as the people, their alms would unto him give.
Silver and gold, have I none, Peter said,
But wrought, in Jesus' name, a miracle instead;
For wher saying, arise up and walk, the lame man
To praise God and leap immediately began.

The excitement of the people over this being great,
Then Peter many truths concerning Jesus did relate;
And multitudes were converted, though some were displeased,
So Peter and John by the soldiers were seized.
Then before the Sanhedrim the next day were brought,
Who to stop their preaching in various ways sought.

But no satisfaction Peter unto them gave,
And told them that Jesus alone was able to save;
He whom they crucified and God raised from the dead,
Although set at nought, was now placed at the head.
Now Peter and John, being both ignorant and unlearned,
That they had been with Jesus, was plainly discerned;
For although being threatened, they no timidity show,
So they dare not do otherwise than let them both go.

And now with their friends, in prayer and in praise,
Their voices together in one accord raise.
Then the building being shaken, to them plainly told
That God was still with them, and made them feel bold.
So they consecrated themselves to Jesus anew,
And their labors more fruitful, constantly grew.

Many of the converts desired the apostles to divide
Their possessions with those whom of means were denied.
But Ananias, having treachery and greed in his heart,
Pretended to give all, and gave only a part.
His wife, Sapphira, to his plan did agree;
But Peter miraculously the whole scheme could see.

And accordingly rebuked them, for attempting to deceive
The Lord Jesus, on whom they had professed to believe.
But they both were punished for their sin and deceit,
For nearly together they fell dead at Peter's feet.
Which caused a great many to tremble with fear,
For, doubtless, there were others like them insincere.

But the truly converted could now plainly see,
That followers of Jesus were John and Peter to be.
So the sick and the afflicted were unto them brought,
And God through Peter many miracles wrought.
But the hatred of the Saducees was very soon shown,
And so into prison the apostles were thrown.

However, in confinement they did not long stay,
But were preaching again the very next day;
For an angel of the Lord came and opened the door,
And told them to preach the same as before.

Of their miraculous escape the chief priests soon hear,
And to do them open violence accordingly fear.

But now they are questioned by the council again,
Who learn that they fear only God and not men.
Also as true witnesses for Jesus they stand,
And intend to obey his every command.
Learning this stirred their anger to such an extent,
That to slay them outright was now by them meant.

But one Gamaliel, a doctor of the law,
The danger of this course immediately saw,
And advised them to let the apostles alone,
Whom, if aided by God, could not be overthrown;
And if not, their work will all come to naught,
Of this substantial proof before them he brought.
And so the apostles were beaten and released,
Also told that their preaching now must be ceased.

But they departed, rejoicing that in Jesus' dear name
They were counted as worthy to thus suffer shame;
Nor did they cease in the temple to preach,
Also in every house they continued to teach.
Until so many to believe on the Lord were inclined,
That a necessity it became at length, so we find,
To appoint seven men, filled with the Holy Ghost,
To assist in ministering to this now mighty host.

Among them was Stephen, who with God's Grace being filled,
Became the first martyr, and by stoning was killed;

For when accused by his enemies, he dared boldly
    proclaim,
As he was now persecuted, so were the prophets the
    same.
And that they who cruelly the dear Lord did kill,
Stiff-necked, were resisting the Holy Ghost still.

And then looking upward into Heaven, he cried,
I see Jesus standing at his Father's right side.
But the anger of his persecutors now was so great,
That for his destruction they no longer could wait.
So out of the city, they now Stephen led,
To be bruised with stones until he was dead.

When dying, this martyr did unto God pray,
This sin to their charge dear Lord do not lay;
But the hearts of these men seemed harder to grow,
For against the whole church their spite they now
    show,
And the most vindictive, we read, of them all
Was a man of Tarsus, at this time called Saul.
His hatred of Christains so intense came to be,
That to other countries for refuge many did flee.

Into Samaria went one, called Philip by name,
Who it seems a successor to Stephen became.
Peter and John of his good works having heard,
Followed, and together they there preached the
    word.
And thousands were converted, Simon with the rest,
Who before an evil spirit must have possessed.
For he bewitched the people and made them believe
That his power from God he did surely receive.

Now the Lord unto Philip spake and did say,
Go down unto Gaza, and so, while on the way,
A man reading the scripture by him was seen—
'Twas an Ethiopian eunuch, an officer of the queen.
To converse with the man Philip being led,
Asked if he understood what he now read.
The eunuch, desiring in Philip to confide,
Invited him with him in the chariot to ride.

Now the way of salvation Philip unto him taught,
Thus to see his necessity the eunuch was brought.
So coming to some water, as they went on their way,
What hindereth me to be baptized? he doth say.
To baptize him Philip now only did wait,
That a confession of faith he might unto him state.

And then he baptized him in Jesus' own name,
When up out of the water both of them came.
Then the spirit of the Lord away Philip bore,
And the eunuch was permitted to see him no more.
But on his way home, now rejoicing he went;
And Philip by the Lord to Azotus was sent.

So in all of the cities he passed through, he preached,
Until Cesarea was at length by him reached.
In all parts the apostles, now met with success:
But in Damascus their work God did especially bless.
Now Saul hearing these things, was greatly displeased,
And so gained permission for the converts to be seized,

Also to be bound and unto Jerusalem brought,
And there to be punished as best it was thought.

And so with some soldiers, Saul started to go
To Damascus, and there his authority show.
Oh, how little he thought that those he despised,
As well beloved brethren so soon would be prized;
But a servant of the Lord, he was destined to be,
For God, in his omnipotence, did so decree.

Thus a voice from Heaven he caused him to hear,
As unto Damascus he was about drawing near.
Which his wickedness brought before him so plain,
That three days from all nourishment he doth abstain,
Also, during this time, he was totally blind,
But afterward restored and in his right mind.

For God knowing that Saul did truly repent,
Ananias a disciple to minister unto him sent.
Then Saul, being filled with the Holy Ghost, did arise,
That some of the apostles, might now, him baptize.
After being converted, a powerful preacher he became,
And we find that Paul is henceforth his name.

The great change in his belief of course enemies made,
And to utterly destroy him were many plots laid:
So the disciples by night, kindly helped him away
From Damascus, where now it was unsafe to stay.
When reaching Jerusalem, the Christians there fear,
That his love for the Saviour is not wholly sincere:

But Barnabas was able their doubts to remove,
For the facts of Paul's conversion could unto them
    prove.
And so unto Tarsus, by the brethren he was brought,
That in his own city the Gospel could be taught.

Now the churches multiplied, and the good work
    went on,
And none were more zealous than Peter and John.
Peter preaching at Lydda, a miracle wrought,
And to believe on the Lord Jesus thus many were
    brought.
Soon after at Joppa, he raised from the dead,
Dorcas, a true Christian, who by charity was led.
For the death of this woman a great many grieve,
And because of the miracle, on Jesus believe.

From Joppa to Cesarea Peter next went,
A Roman Centurion after him having sent.
'Twas Cornelius, who, devout, a vision did behold,
And to send for Peter, by God's angel was told,
Also a vision by Peter not long after was seen,
Showing that with God there was no difference
    between
Gentile or Jew, bond men or free,
But all nations converted he desired to see.

And then as Cornelius' servants unto Peter drew
    near,
From the Spirit again these words he doth hear:
Peter, behold, three men are seeking for thee,
So arise up and go, for they were sent here by me.

And so to meet Cornelius he went and there found,
That his kinsmen and friends had gathered around,
And as well as Cornelius, very anxious appear,
God's precious truths now from him to hear.

So all about Jesus he does unto them tell,
And upon all those that heard the Holy Ghost fell.
Some Jews being present, were greatly surprised,
But Peter, nevertheless had the believers baptized.
For that God was no respecter of persons he perceived;
And all could be saved that on him truly believed.

Now king Herod began the church to persecute,
And killed James, an Apostle, which did the Jews suit.
Then Peter he intended should share the same fate
But put him in prison, after the passover to wait.
To pray for his escape the church did not cease,
Notwithstanding were surprised on seeing his release.
For Peter, immediately, when into the prison cast,
Between two soldiers with chains was made fast.

But with God there is nothing too hard nor too great,
And so he sent an angel, Peter now to liberate.
With horror at his escape the guards were all filled,
For they rightly conjectured, Herod would order them killed.
But this wicked king did not long them survive,
For we read that by worms he was eaten alive.

About this time the church to Antioch sent
Barnabas, who to Tarsus first after Paul went.

Then together at Antioch they preached for a year,
And the disciples as Christians first were spoken of here.
Now Barnabas and Paul by the Holy Ghost sent,
To preach the Gospel of Christ, to different places went.
At the city of Paphos, 'twas the deputy's desire,
The way of Salvation of them to inquire;
But Elymas, a sorcerer, sought to poison his mind,
And in punishment, for a season, was made totally blind.
Then Paulus, the deputy, because of the miracle wrought,
To accept the Lord Jesus was immediately brought.

And now Paul and Barnabas back to Antioch were led;
But Mark being with them, went to Jerusalem instead.
In the synagogues at Antioch, Paul and Barnabas taught
That the Gospel to the Gentiles was sure to be brought.
The history of the prophets, Paul recited also;
And the perversity of the Jews he plainly did show.
But this consolation he unto them gave,
That Jesus was able and willing to save.

Now the gentiles believed, also desired of Jesus to learn,
But the Jews with blasphemy the Gospel did spurn,

And stirred up the people against the evangelists, we read,
Until in expelling them both they finally succeed.
So they went to Iconium, where both Jew and Greek,
The way of salvation are led earnestly to seek.

But after a time, the unbelieving Jews,
Did Paul and Barnabas so despitefully use,
That they fled to Lystra, and there healed a lame man,
So the people to worship them immediately began.
But both Paul and Barnabas now bade them refrain,
And that their allegiance was to God, tried to explain;
Which against Paul, especially, so stirred up their ire,
That, with other unbelievers, to take his life they conspire.
So together they stoned him until dead, as they thought,
But again unto life, by God's power, he was brought.

Now through western Asia Minor Paul and Barnabas go,
And although persecuted, no less ardor show;
But great dissensions, regarding circumcision now arose,
And men from Judea, unto Paul and Barnabas propose

That they should prepare to go to Jerusalem, and see
If the apostles and elders there with them agree.
So they went, and brought with them on their return,
Barnabas and Silas, their message to confirm.

Who letters of greeting unto the converted Gentiles there gave,
And assured them God's grace could alone their souls save.
For without change of heart, all else was as naught,
For thus the Lord Jesus unto his disciples had taught.
And so of good works let us none think to boast;
Since God knowing the heart has given the Holy Ghost
Alike unto Gentiles, as well as the Jews,
Who to believe on his son do not refuse.
Now to continue in Antioch, Paul and Barnabas decide,
And Silas was pleased with them there to abide.
But after a time, to Barnabas said Paul,
At the places we have preached let us now again call;
Barnabas immediately consented, but with this proviso,
John, surnamed Mark, was with them to go.
But to this proposition, Paul would not consent,
So Silas in the place of Barnabas went.

Then Barnabas at liberty, took with him Mark,
And together for Cyprus the two did embark.

But Paul and Silas through Syria and Cilicia went,
To confirm there the churches being their intent.
Then coming to Lystra, Paul decided to take
A disciple called Timothy, of him a companion to make.
So preaching in the cities they pass on their way,
The churches are increased in numbers each day.
And at Troas a vision to Paul did appear,
Come to Macedonia and help us, he plainly doth hear.

So they sailed for Philippi, and on the Sabbath day,
Went out of the city, by the river to pray.
Hearing their devotions, a certain woman then came,
Who was a seller of purple, Lydia by name:
Paul told her of Jesus, and his power to save,
And so gladly her heart she unto him gave.
Then being baptized, and her whole household also,
To abide in her home she constrained them to go.

And while in Lydia's home they continued to remain,
A damsel, who by soothsaying brought her master great gain,
Followed them about, until Paul with pity being led,
In Jesus' own name, to the evil spirit said—
Come out of the woman, and in the same hour,
The damsel was relieved, also knew Jesus' power.

But the anger of her master with vengeance did fall,
On the innocent heads of Silas and Paul.
Who caused them to be beaten, and into prison cast,
While their feet in the stocks were also made fast.

But this trial of faith with Christian fortitude they
  bear,
And at midnight praise God in song and in prayer.
Then suddenly the walls of the prison did shake,
And the doors were opened by a tremendous earth-
  quake.

Now the keeper supposing the prisoners had fled,
Drew out his sword his own blood to shed.
Do no harm to thyself, cried Paul, we are here;
Then trembling, the keeper fell down with fear.
Now what shall I do to be saved? he doth call;
Believe on the Lord Jesus Christ, answered Paul.

And then he and Silas did further explain,
How life everlasting each and all might attain.
So the keeper and his family were baptized right
  away,
Also Silas and Paul were released the next day.
For the magistrates, learning they were Romans,
  greatly fear
Lest the prisoners for malpractice should against
  them appear.

But Paul and Silas, in Philippi, now only did stay,
A few words of comfort unto the brethren to say;
And then to Thessalonica they went, and three days
They preached of the Saviour and his wonderful
  ways.
Many Gentiles were converted, and also some Jews,
But the unbelieving ones did them despitefully use.

They even assaulted the house of Jason, the friend,
Upon whose hospitality Paul and Silas depend.

But he with other brethren managed so well,
That no further harm the apostles befell.
And so now, safely by night, Berea they reach,
Where the Jews in the synagogue allow them to preach.
And many were converted, but their enemies coming now,
That Paul should remain peacefully they would not allow.

So advised by friends, he decided for Athens to leave,
Where the idolatry of the people caused him to grieve:
Against their sacrilegiousness, Paul declaimed every day,
Also told them of Jesus, and of salvation the way.
Very strange to the wise men this doctrine doth appear,
And yet they are anxious more of it to hear.

So in the midst of Mars' Hill they all congregate,
That the precious truths of the Bible Paul may relate.
Who spake first of God and then his dear Son,
How he suffered and died, to redeem every one.
But when hearing that Jesus had risen from the dead,
We will hear thee again, some of them said.

Some mockingly scoffed, and others believed his report,
Among whom was Dionysius, a member of the court.

Now to go to Corinth, Paul is led to decide,
And with a Jew and his wife is permitted to abide;
While in the synagogue, every Sabbath he earnestly seeks
To lead to the Saviour both the Jews and the Greeks.
Although meeting opposition, many of the Corinthians believed,
And being baptized, the Holy Ghost then received.
For a year and a half Paul at this place did remain,
As God in a vision promised him there to sustain.
Therefore, when persecuted, he came to no harm,
For underneath and about him was the Everlasting Arm.

At length leaving Corinth, Paul to Ephesus went,
And to accompany him there, Priscilla and Aquilla consent.
These Jewish friends from Corinth were the same,
With whom he had lived, and now his helpers became.
Now the Gospel three years at Ephesus Paul taught,
Also wonderful miracles by him were wrought.
So many were converted, and pretenders were led
To renounce their profession and serve God instead.

Among the false gods, to which these people bowed down,
Was one called Diana, the greatest in renown;
Silver shrines for this goddess were by silversmiths made,
And by the people different prices for them were paid.

Paul rebuked them now for their idolatry and sin,
And so to persecute him they then did begin.

And had not the town clerk their anger appeased,
Paul would have no doubt now by them been seized.
But peace being restored, he decided to depart;
So embracing his companions, for Macedonia did start.
And in the different cities he taught them again,
That God sent his Son to be the Saviour of men.

And now unto Troas, in Asia, being led,
He restored a young man to life who was dead;
He also observed the Lord's supper while there,
And talked with the people of their eternal welfare.
But wishing to be in Jerusalem at Pentecost day,
Not long in any place must he now stay.

And now to sail by Ephesus, being his intent,
For the elders to come to Miletus he sent,
That words of counsel, he could unto them speak,
And adjure them for the good of their churches to seek.
For after his departure he said he well knew,
Grievous persecutions they were sure to pass through.

Of his own work among them he spake in this way,
The whole counsel of God I was fearless to say
Unto both Jew and Gentile, although it offend,
I kept nothing back that would profit in the end.
And now going to Jerusalem, uncertain of my fate,
The commands of the Lord I only await.
Neither unto myself, my life I hold dear,
If only faithful at last, before Jesus I appear.

I shall see you no more, he also doth say,
Then kneeling, he with them did fervently pray.

'Twas a sorrowful parting, but saddest of all,
That never again were the brethren to see Paul;
Who from the city of Miletus, now sailing away,
Stopped first in Tyre, there a few words to say.
Then coming to Cesarea, with Philip he abode,
The same who with the Eunuch in the chariot rode.

And so while he tarried, the prophet Agabus came there,
Who was led grievous things unto him to declare—
Concerning Jerusalem and the unconverted Jews,
Who would bind and otherwise him despitefully use.
His companions, on hearing this prophecy, wept,
But from going to Jerusalem Paul could not be kept.

For he said, I am ready to be bound and to die
For *His* sake, whom these Jews did once crucify.
So then at Cesarea, Paul no longer did stay,
But went with some brethren to Jerusalem straightway,
And on his arrival was joyfully received,
By all whom on God and his Son Jesus believed.

But entering the Temple, to preach, then some Jews,
Of blasphemy and annulling the laws him accuse;
And so now from the Temple, Paul was thrust out,
And would then have been killed without any doubt,
Had not the chief captain with some soldiers appeared,
And with their violent treatment of him interfered;

But that he should be bound was the captain's command,
Until the whole truth they could fully understand.

And when learning that Paul was a Jew and not Greek,
He gave him permission of his history to speak.
So the story of his conversion in Hebrew he told,
Nor no truth of importance did he seek to withhold,
While his accusers all listened with seeming content,
Until speaking of the Gentiles and to them being sent;
But this caused the hearts of these wicked men
To be filled with anger and jealousy again.

Now the Captain learning that Paul was born free,
Knew well that as a Roman, protected he must be;
And although before the council now he was taken,
By the soldiers he was protected, nor was he forsaken
By God, who spake unto him, be of good cheer,
For in Rome thou shalt testify as thou hast done here.

And so to Cesarea, at last, Paul was sent,
For his enemies to kill him were certainly bent.
A letter was written to Felix, the governor, also,
By the captain, designing Paul's innocence to show.
And so the governor asking some questions of Paul,
Commanded him placed in the king's judgment hall.

Then in five days after, from Jerusalem there came,
Ananias, with a lawyer, Tertullus by name,

So now Paul's case before the governor was brought,
And to condemn him his accusers eagerly sought;
But Paul, when permitted, an account to them gave
Of Jesus, and his mission the whole world to save.

So although a prisoner, great liberty had Paul,
And on the governor and his wife was invited to call.
While there Felix trembled, when of the judgment he spake,
But yet wished for more time, his preparations to make.
Still with him, he communed, very often we read,
Until Festus, in two years, did him succeed.

And then immediately of him the Jews came and sought
That Paul for a trial to Jerusalem could be brought.
And so at Cesarea was Paul now again
Brought up for trial before the same men.
But being unable, as before, at this time,
Of proving him guilty of committing any crime,
Something more must be done, and so they decide,
That in Jerusalem or Rome he next must be tried.

To choose for himself was his privilege, and so,
He said before Cesar, to Rome, he would go.
But ere his departure, to visit Festus there came,
Bernice and Agrippa, the latter a king of some fame.
Who hearing Paul's case, said to Festus that he
Was anxious the prisoner to both hear and see.

And so an excuse for a new trial they seek,
When Paul was permitted, as usual, to speak;

And so forcibly by him was Jesus portrayed,
That Agrippa to accept him he did almost persuade.
And were not his case now left in Cæsar's hands,
Festus would gladly have made loose his bands.

But with other prisoners, he was soon sent away,
Arriving in Rome, after a lengthy delay
Caused by a shipwreck, which Paul could foresee,
But the Master with him was not willing to agree,
And so Paul's advice, all unheeded, was given,
While the ship in the storm to destruction was driven.

But the angel of God, unto Paul did appear,
Saying none shall be lost, so be of good cheer,
But on a certain island, you all shall be cast,
Nevertheless, before Cæsar be brought at the last.
Paul believing the message every word to be true,
Now spake cheering words unto all the ship's crew.
The storm having continued fourteen nights, so we read,
Both rest and food the sailors all need;
So Paul now besought them to partake of some meat,
And after giving thanks, he sat with them to eat.

Now the ship going to pieces, the sailors suggest,
The prisoners should be killed, their escape to arrest;
But the centurion in charge, desiring to save Paul,
So commanded a chance to be given to all.
And thus the whole crew came safely to land,
Being kept also guided by God's loving hand.

The chief of the island, was Publius, whom we find.
Was unto the crew both courteous and kind;

But Paul was permitted, by the help of the Lord,
The kindness of the people to amply reward,
For during the three months on the island they stayed,
Many sick unto death by his prayers were whole made.

So when leaving the island they were nothing denied,
But with every necessary by the people supplied,
And when reaching Rome Paul was gladly received,
By all whom on Jesus as their Saviour believed.
Also he was permitted with one soldier to live,
Which privilege the officers did unto him give.

Now the chief of the Jews before Paul did appear,
Who proved his innocence so plain and so clear;
That he was invited to preach, but then, as to-day,
Some believed and others grieved the Spirit away.
Two years in Rome Paul preached and did dwell;
But of his life after this not much can we tell.
His epistles, so loving, helpful and sublime,
Were written we know not where or what time.

But this matters not, so long as we know
They were written, a blessing on all to bestow.
For if these Divine precepts we study and obey,
Into the joy of our Lord we shall enter some day.
What more can we ask, what greater reward,
Than forever to be with Christ Jesus, the Lord.

The last book in the Bible, Revelations we call,
And we find it the greatest enigma of all.

The writer was St. John, who, persecuted in Jesus' name,
An exile on the island of Patmos became.
But inspired by God, he was permitted to behold,
Many glorious visions which of Heavenly things told.
Also the bottomless pit, and all earthly things,
Jesus to his vision at different times brings.

But dear readers how precious the thought that God's grace
Is sufficient to save the whole human race
From this perpetual darkness, which in vision John saw,
Since Jesus has fulfilled, for believers, the law.
Also his precious blood shed, that the children of men,
Although under a curse, might through him live again.

Oh how loving and kind the dear Saviour must be,
To suffer and die, thus to save such as we.
Then shall we reject him? just think of the cost—
A soul without Jesus forever is lost.
Then come and accept him in Christ's stead we entreat,
For how joyful 'twill be in Heaven to meet:

> There to live right on forever,
> There to part again, no never.
> There where all is joy and love,
> We may reign with Christ above.

THE END.

www.ingramcontent.com/pod-product-compliance
Lightning Source LLC
Chambersburg PA
CBHW021410230426
43666CB00006B/693